Treasure
in
Clay Jars

Treasure in Clay Jars

*Personal Stories
of Faith
from Indiana
United Methodists
told in their
own words*

Edited by
Lynne Bevan DeMichele

PROVIDENCE HOUSE PUBLISHERS
Franklin, Tennessee

Printed in the United States of America

02   01   00   99   98   1   2   3   4   5

Library of Congress Catalog Card Number: 98-65828

ISBN: 1-57736-101-6

Cover design by Gary Bozeman

PROVIDENCE HOUSE PUBLISHERS
238 Seaboard Lane • Franklin, Tennessee 37067
800-321-5692

*T*o those
whose faith stories
are yet to be told.

Contents

FOREWORD   ix

PREFACE   xi

INTRODUCTION   xiii

PART ONE—CERTAIN WONDERS   3

A Lie at the Altar • Asleep at the Wheel • The Bird in the
Window • The Brass Deer • Fireflies • God Chooses •
Golden Circle • Healing Touch • "Jesus Freak" • Night
Light • Night Messenger • With Open Arms • Summer of
Separation • The Right Child • The Seventh Wave •
Unexpected Calls • What Matters

PART TWO—PRAYER, ANSWERED AND OTHERWISE   27

After Forty Years, a Prayer • Chewing Up Anger • In God's
Time • Mountain Dreams • One Kind of Genuine Miracle •
Praying for Parents • Strong Medicine • Stubborn Streak •
Miracle Girl • Waiting for Hope • What Adam Really Saw

PART THREE—UNEXPECTED ANGELS   43

Crowd of Angels • A Tough Nut to Crack • Candles for a
Dismal Soul • Christ as a Bag Lady • For the Love of Mark
• Heroes, Guardians and God • Holy Hands • Kindred
Spirits • Mother's Hands • My Angel Swims • Samaritan in
a Truck • Stepping Out on Faith • The Kayla Connection •
Two on a God Quest

PART FOUR — THE MANY SHADES OF GRACE   65

A Miracle to Deliver • After the Killing • An Answer on the Sand • Flowers under Snow • Following the White Fields • Heart Sparks • Pickup Full of Blessings • Sanctuary • Sin of Omission • Standing on the Promises • Sunflower Colors • The Color of Brotherhood • The Electric Train

PART FIVE — IN THE CRUCIBLE   85

Blessed Assurance • Bullies • Coping Alone? • Corn Supper • From One Trapeze • Full Circle • Husband, Son and Holy Light • The Beauty of the Scars • When It Rains, It Pours • Whispering Hope • Why Can't I Walk, God?

PART SIX — OUT OF THE DARKNESS   101

All the Promises • Changing the Course of a River • Come Home, My Son • Faith x 3 = 6 • Falling into Grace • God and Good Business • Leaving Is Not an Option • Lower Lights Burning • I Once Was Lost • One True Friend • Pumpkin Pie Memories • The Last Bell • Wrapped in Love

PART SEVEN — MOMENTS OF HOLY BEAUTY   119

A Heart for Glass • Amid Soldiers & Hymns • Assurance Alive! • A Bouquet of Trust • Bringing Church • Every Common Bush Afire • Hill Country Pieta • Over in That Bright Light • Rainbow 'Round the Moon • Song in the Night • Unbelievers' Salvation • A Night without Stars • Unbroken Circle

AUTHOR/TITLE INDEX   139
ABOUT THE COVER   146

Foreword

Whatever else it means to be a Christian disciple, telling one's story of faith—a testimony, if you will—is at the core of such meaning. Early followers were encouraged to go and tell what they had seen and heard. They were also instructed on other occasions to tell what had happened to them as a result of an encounter with Jesus.

There is nothing quite as compelling as sharing one's story. Especially is this so when bearing testimony to those outside the faith community. Who is Christ? What does it mean to be a believer? What difference does faith make in an increasingly secularized society? What role does faith play in the everyday challenge of living? To answer these questions in simple convincing words always captures the listener.

Many faithful disciples are reluctant to tell their story. Some by temperament are more inclined to be introverted, even fearing misunderstanding. For these servants, life and deed become their story. For others to tell the story is to relive its impact and further strengthen faith. There is a special value to putting one's story in writing. It gives wings to go beyond place, time and audience.

In this volume, Indiana Christians of The United Methodist Church share their stories. Some will make you laugh or cry, ponder

and reflect. Insights are shared, doubts bared, joys and hopes celebrated. There will be times when the reader will say "Amen." Other
times, one will simply wonder. But always these stories of faith point to
hope and praise . . . and challenge. God becomes more real, faith more
central and the world more friendly as each writer tells his story and
tells her story.

    May you be inspired and encouraged to tell your own story!

Woodie W. White
Bishop, Indiana Area
The United Methodist Church
February 9, 1998

Preface

For it is the God who said,
"Let light shine out of darkness,"
who has shone in our hearts to give the light
of the knowledge of the glory of God
in the face of Jesus Christ.
But we have this
treasure in clay jars,
so that it may be made clear that this
extraordinary power belongs to God
and does not come from us.

2 Corinthians 4:6–7 (NRSV)

Introduction

On December 17, 1997, I was diagnosed with breast cancer. The day after Christmas I had a modified radical mastectomy. My life changed forever.

But my story really began on a cold, rainy day in March, nine months earlier. I am a United Methodist minister. I had just attended a church-related meeting. Walking to my car, I really questioned whether the church had a future. I was frustrated, angry and sad. Complaining, I told myself, really wasn't an answer to the dilemma. It rarely is. So, for several nights I offered my grumblings and concerns to God as I prayed for some kind of illumination.

In the wee hours of the morning I awakened, remembering the story of a mother who lost her son and how she overcame depression and loneliness, of a man convicted of fraud and, through a dramatic life change, went back into prisons to help others, and of a victim of incest who conquered despair and, through her profession, now encourages others to grow and live fulfilling lives. I recalled numerous occasions when ordinary people entrusted their extraordinary stories of hope and courage, of strength and joy to me. That was the inauguration of an idea to encourage Hoosier United Methodists to tell their stories to the world.

I invited a handful of people I barely knew to join me for lunch and a time of getting acquainted. I told them about my rainy day meeting and my early morning experience. That started a chain of events that culminated in the writing of this book. Every time we gathered as a vision team, we shared our personal stories with one another. I came to love and appreciate Lynne DeMichele, Minnietta Millard and Walter Mayer as we listened to the happenings in each other's lives and how we were touched by God in one way or another.

We were well into the editing process when I received the news that I had cancer. I was overwhelmed with shock and fear, grief and loss. When the word got out of my impending surgery, churches and individuals all over Indiana and beyond began praying for me. Cards, flowers, food and calls poured in. Literally thousands of prayers were being offered on my behalf. I could never have imagined receiving such an outpouring of love. And through those difficult days, I discovered a deeper place in my own soul—a resource so deep that in it I began to heal and find joy. On January 27 my oncologist announced that I was cured with just a 3 percent chance of a metastasis. He sent me home saying, "Go home and live a good life." That's my story.

This book contains the stories of many other United Methodists who are living life in the trenches and discovering the wonders of faith. I am grateful to them. As you listen to their stories, my hope is you will be inspired to share your own.

Andrea Leininger

Treasure in Clay Jars

Part One

CERTAIN WONDERS

A Lie at the Altar

Sue Jackson Hawks

Knightstown

My older sister Bernice and I were fifteen and fourteen when we plowed corn in the rich soil in Illinois with our Dad, John Jared and older brother, Dennis. There were also three sisters: Kathryn, five; Mildred, two; and Dorothy, one. We helped take care of them in the evening.

Those were long, hot days, but Dad planned for a long noon hour to give us some rest. Our grandmother lived with us part of the time when we were small, and she read the Bible to us. At bedtime Dad, Mom, Grandma, and Dennis knelt at their chairs. Bernice and I knelt with our elbows in our little red rocking chairs while Dad prayed for his family.

When the corn plowing was finished, Bernice and I worked in the garden with Mom. She would warn us never to be jealous, because it is the sin that leads to all other sins. She stressed that we must be saved.

When we moved to this new community, we knew we would go to church the first Sunday. It was March and the roads were muddy. On Saturday, our neighbor drug the road from our house to a nine-foot cement road leading to the church, and Sunday morning the ground was frozen making it a smooth road to travel. He was a Presbyterian and we were Methodists. The two churches worshipped together, alternating Sundays. The Methodist minister served both churches. The minister and his wife took turns preaching Sunday morning and evening, as she was also a minister. They sang beautiful duets. Each Sunday I heard "Narrow is the gate to heaven and broad is the road to destruction and few there be who enter heaven's gate. Come to the altar and get saved." If someone had quoted some salvation scripture, I would have gone.

Each day in the field, I talked to God and told him I didn't want to go to hell. My worry kept me from hearing him if he was trying to give me a message. One Sunday morning Bernice stepped out in the aisle and I followed her to the altar. We were the only ones at the altar and all I could think about was everyone in the pews watching me. If the minister prayed for me or quoted scripture, I didn't hear it. All I heard was "Do you feel better?" Finally, I said "Yes," so I could get out of there. People came by and shook our hands. Bernice and I didn't discuss it, so I don't know if she found the Lord at that time or if it was later. I felt terrible that I lied.

After about a year, I said "Okay Lord, if you want me to go to hell, I'll just go there because I can't do a thing about it." Maybe six months later when the congregation was singing, I felt a heavy weight being pulled up from each foot through my body and out the top of my head. I remember thinking, where did it go? I looked up to see a cloud with a tail going out the side door by the altar. I felt light as a feather, but I didn't tell anyone for years. Recently, Kathryn told me that she was five years old when Bernice and I went to the altar. She wanted to go then but didn't. The next Sunday she and a friend went and she had a wonderful experience. Even though I lied at the altar, the Lord used that time to bring Kathryn and others to him.

I'm eighty-five and I can look back at how the Lord has blessed, protected, and led me through those years. Another story!

Asleep at the Wheel

Loretta Spilker
Indianapolis

I was exhausted as I piled into the car. True to form, I had been "burning my candle at both ends" and was not looking forward to the eleven-hour drive home. Since moving out to North Carolina, I had adopted the pattern of driving back and forth to Indianapolis twice a year—Christmas and summer vacation. Though I eagerly looked forward to visiting with family and friends, there were just so many to see in one short week (I am truly blessed), so my vacation schedule was always a hectic one with very little time for any real R & R.

Happy but tired, I began the long journey home. An hour into the drive, I was already looking forward to my first fifteen-minute break. The drive was actually eleven hours and forty-five minutes if you count the three fifteen minute breaks I always took to get some gas and stretch a bit. At the first stop I jogged around the rest area. Why do I always have to push myself? I asked. I had no reply. Windows down, stereo blaring, shoveling down popcorn and coke, I made it to the second stop. While I gassed up the car I sent up a quick but heartfelt prayer. "Dear God, please get me home safe and sound!"

Back on the road again, the inevitable finally happened and no amount of wind, noise, food or caffeine could prevent it. . . . I fell asleep at the wheel.

Now, this was no ordinary little nod at the wheel followed by a quick head jerk up. We're talkin' "catchin' some ZZZZ's," "sawin' logs," "countin' sheep." I was *asleep* at the wheel. I have no idea how long I slept, but I awoke with a start (It's always startling to wake up with your hands at the wheel of a car, wouldn't you agree!) and, of course, immediately looked around me to see where I was. Looking left, I was surprised to see a car *right next* to mine. Looking to the right, I found the same thing! Next, a quick look in the rear view mirror. Much to my surprise, there were three cars right on my tail! (Actually, one was right behind me and the other two were right behind the cars to the left and right of me.)

I was horrified, fully awake. With my heart pounding and my blood racing, the only thing I could think of was, "Oh my gosh! I'm endangering the lives of all these poor people! I've gotta get outta here, NOW!" I hit the accelerator and shot out of that six-pack of cars like a bat out of hell.

Wanting to see how much distance I'd put between me and the poor, innocent bystanders, I looked once more in my rear view mirror. My mouth dropped to the floor. I saw nothing but a deserted highway! "What in the world?" I exclaimed to myself. "They were just there!" My eyes combed the deserted highway once again. In the last few seconds I hadn't passed an exit, gone around a bend, or over a hill. Where in the world did they go? I asked myself again. That's when I finally realized the error in my thinking. They hadn't gone anywhere in the world! In the blink of an eye, they had gone back up to heaven! Tears coursing down my cheeks, I thanked God for sending my guardian angel to my rescue.

Even today, my eyes well with tears at the memory of my close encounter with my guardian angel and his friends. Still burning my candle at both ends, my hands confidently grip the steering wheel as I drive along this road we call "life," because I *know* that God isn't just along for the ride!

The Bird in the Window

Pamela Haase
Indianapolis

It was a dreary March day full of cold rain and gray clouds. It was a time of struggle and loss. My divorce was final, and the reality of the pain was overwhelming. I, like so many other people, felt as though I would never have to face divorce; but there I was—divorced, and just several months after I had sold my Independent Insurance Agency. What was an excellent business decision left me without an office, staff and wonderful group of clients. I was now a single, unemployed parent of three teenagers.

My secretary had a home on a lake that had always been a sanctuary to me. She loaned me the key to go spend a couple of days to be alone and start the process of healing. It seemed to take forever to drive to the cabin. What was normally a pleasant trip was filled with hopeless feelings and tears. By the time I arrived at the cabin all I wanted to do was sleep. I had never felt so tired in all my life.

As I was starting to unpack, there was a horrible crash. Startled, I turned quickly in the direction of the noise. Then it happened again, louder yet. I could finally see a female robin had become confused by her reflection and kept flying into the bedroom window. She would fly away and then instantly turn and fly, repeatedly crashing into the window. By this point I was angry at the bird and God. I was not even allowed peace in my sanctuary. I had no feeling for the bird, only pity for myself.

She began hitting the window with such force that there were traces of her blood left behind on the glass. With the sight of her blood, I began to stop thinking of myself and to think of her. It seemed that she had been hitting the window forever, and the poor thing was destroying herself. Somehow God gave me the grace to realize that the bird was doing only what she knew to do. She had only the one reflection of herself. It was that reflection that would destroy her. How many times had I been like that in my life, that I only knew of myself in one role traveling in one direction? Many times it is in living in that identity and not ourselves that is our destruction, and yet we return to the same reflection.

It seemed like an eternity before I realized that I could stop the reflection and light her a new way. When I turned on the bedroom lamp, she saw through the window and chose another direction. She turned and flew away.

A dear friend called me later that day to see if I was going to be all right. I shared with him the sign that God had made visible to me. We were both touched with the stark reality of what I had experienced.

It has been years since that day. I have had many joyful and sad moments—my sweet miseries. Life has been full and very rewarding. After years of being single, raising the children and having a busy career, I recently remarried.

I wish I could say that every time I feel sadness or loss, I think of the bird in the window. But, I am sure that I do not remember as often as I should.

When life's transitions and struggles come my way for a moment, I try to remember to look beyond the reflection and see the light. The same light that female robin saw that day, as she turned to fly in a new reflection of herself.

The Brass Deer

Susan J. Elkins
Indianapolis

My husband of twenty-four years passed away August of 1986. After two and a half years of suffering from a rare spinal cancer, he was taken to a much better place. Before cancer, Bob was a very active entrepreneur who enjoyed nature and all the simple things in life. Through surgeries, being hospitalized for many months at two hospitals in Indiana and two hospitals in New York, and in the end being paralyzed, he always maintained a wonderful spirit. It was the little things that helped us through these times. Once a friend brought three beagle puppies to visit Bob and put them in bed with him. That was his favorite dog. Another friend wore a clown wig to the hospital to cheer him. The outpouring of love from our friends, family and church was so moving. We had all hoped for a miracle of life.

When the day came to make arrangements after his death, my children and I were leaving the funeral home and had decided to go find the grave site. When we arrived at the site my children said "Look!" There was a large buck leaping across the cemetery into a wooded area. It was so beautiful; it was something Bob would have enjoyed seeing.

On returning home that day a friend came to bring food and check on us. I shared seeing the deer with her and she said "Go get your Bible and look up 2 Samuel 22:33–34." It reads, "It is God who arms me with strength and makes my way perfect. He makes my feet like the feet of a deer, he enables me to stand on the height." What comfort those words were for me. God had reminded me that he is my strength.

Two days later at the funeral home we had received many planters and beautiful flowers, but later on in the day I was handed a small box and in the box were two brass deer, one with its head to the ground the other looking up to heaven. It was a simple gift from my friend that had me look up the Bible verse.

It has been ten years since his death and the brass deer are upon my mantle to remind me that God is my strength.

Fireflies

Lucille Singley
Lafayette

One very warm evening in July 1996, my daughter called me to come outside. We walked over to a corner of the hay field which was several acres in size surrounded by trees. As far as we could see the air was completely filled with fireflies. They were having such a good time flashing on and off their mysterious lights in such a playful manner.

The full moon was doing its part by shining down and electrifying the air. Not a sound could be heard, although thousands and thousands were flying over the field and way up into the treetops. Not one was competing for air space. They were flying in complete harmony with each other. Joy, peace and contentment filled the air.

Coming back to the house there seemed to be a voice saying, "Heaven is like that, so quiet and so beautiful, full of joy, peace and happiness." I was reminded of Matthew 6:28, "Consider the lilies of the field, they toil not neither do they spin: and yet I say unto you that Solomon in all his glory was not arrayed like one of these."

There is a statement in Bishop Woodie White's Book, *Conversations of the Heart* that I very much like and it sums up my experience. "Consider the extraordinary in the ordinary things in life."

God Chooses

Diana Yakimchick
Indianapolis

"He leadeth me, he leadeth me; by his own hand he leadeth me." How often I have sung this refrain in church throughout my life without understanding the power of God's leading each and every day. But with the help and understanding love of a very close lady pastor friend, I have become aware of the many ways God's leading transforms my life.

I'm sure many of us remember speech classes from high school or college where we spent hours and hours gathering information to complete a speech assignment and then worried too much about how we looked or what the other students thought to do justice to the actual speech itself. I, personally, had not yet come to the realization that the answer to my jumbled thoughts was God and that he was only a prayer away.

About three years ago, with the encouragement and help of my friend, I found myself in classes again—this time as a student to be a lay speaker for our church. Once again, the classes were easy and enjoyable—but the test came when our senior pastor asked me to fill in for him and deliver a sermon one Sunday while he was going to be on vacation. What would I write about, how would I put it all together, and would I be able to stand in front of my church peers and deliver a message with words that would reach parishioners' hearts as well as their ears?

With the ongoing renewal of my life as a Christian and the encouragement from my friend, I knew that the answers to these questions would come from God. I have learned that my personal responsibility is to continually pray first (about all matters), to read and search the scriptures, and to listen for God's leading.

Within a few days I found myself remembering one particular scripture, John 15:16: "You did not choose me, I chose you. . . ." God had chosen me! And if he had chosen me, he would give me the words to say in a sermon and the ability to deliver them.

As I began writing, the words and phrases seemed to appear on their own at the touch of my fingers on the computer keyboard. I continued my prayer vigil and immersed myself in reading his Word, listening for his direction. I was able to not only write this sermon and deliver it, but have been able to continue this form of witnessing as a substitute pastor in another church. And with this experience I have also been led to lead a women's retreat and to teach Bible study classes in my home church.

As a United Methodist Lay Speaker, I not only feel a strong sense of purpose and fulfillment with these speaking and leading challenges, but I also feel a responsibility in sharing with others the rewards of listening for God's direction through prayer and scripture reading. My gratitude to a caring and loving pastor goes beyond what words can express as I pray daily to be able to accept the challenges God encourages me to accept in witnessing his love to others through his leading of me.

Golden Circle

Jean LaRue
Frankfort

Isabel is a wonderfully kind, quiet, sweet person. She belongs to the adult Sunday School class my husband and I have attended for about thirty years. Even though we have moved away, I think of her often and am grateful for her Christian friendship, cards, and love.

After knowing her for many years, I began to call her Mary-Martha. Isabel has chosen the best portions of each of these biblical women.

On a beautiful June 8, 1988, my husband and I went to a nearby city for his annual heart stress test. After three-plus hours under the scrutiny of heart specialists he received a good report. Going to a nearby Jewish delicatessen for lunch, I enjoyed a wonderful corned beef sandwich with dill pickle and brown mustard. My favorite!

We lived about fifty miles away. En route home, I became ill. With each ten miles, I was more uncomfortable.

Dr. Tom examined me and scheduled gall bladder surgery for later. The next morning I was becoming jaundiced, so was taken to surgery right away. Dr. Tom told my husband that I had pancreatitis. This would be a rather long recovery.

Isabel was so faithful to come. She knew what I needed. Prayer! She often came and said very little; she would sit and hold my hand. Around July 1 she was sitting across from me and praying silently. A beautiful aura, a golden circle came all around us. It was as though God was sprinkling gold dust around us. This was a wonderful sign to me.

"Surely the presence of the Lord is in this place."

After fifty-one days in the hospital, I was able to go home. I am very grateful to God, Dr. Tom, my husband, Isabel, our two pastors and Christian family and friends who prayed for me.

Healing Touch

Suzanne Metzger
Fishers

I was raised by my dyed-in-the-wool Southern Baptist grandmother. I grew up hearing about heaven and an afterlife. I looked at all the miracles on earth and believed there was an afterlife. I missed the passing of family and friends and hoped to see them again in that afterlife. Hoping and believing are good, but knowing is even better. Now, I know.

About two months after my husband and I were married, I discovered that I had breast cancer. I had the first surgery and found out there were malignancies. The second surgery revealed it had spread, and to help ensure survival, I would have to go through chemotherapy, radiation therapy and hormone therapy.

After the second surgery and more incisions, I decided to sleep in the guest room to avoid my husband accidentally rolling onto me. It also allowed me to think things through and semi-plan how I would handle things.

For those of you unfamiliar with this disease, and I sincerely hope that is the majority of you, it follows a very similar pattern in people. It usually goes from breast cancer, to bone cancer, to brain cancer. And, when it goes to bone cancer, it likes to attack the small, fragile ribs.

Now, as I lay there in the guest room thinking about what lay ahead, an incident happened that literally changed my life. All of a sudden, I felt a large, icy hand with pointed steel fingers grabbing hold of my rib cage. I was terrified. I screamed out loud, "Lord, get this evil away from me, please." Then while wide awake and lying on my back, I felt a huge hand—the width of my body—touch the back of my head and run the full length of the back of my body. When this hand reached my rib cage, it pushed the icy steel fingers away from me.

As so many people have said before, an incredible sense of peace came over me, and from that moment on, I knew two things for sure: that I would be all right whatever I had to go through, and that there is another life out there.

I won't know for quite some time if I was touched by the Lord, a guardian angel, or a family member come back to protect me. What I do know is that there is a power far greater than us out there, and it is protecting us on earth.

"Jesus Freak"

Vicki Dodge
Sullivan

Nancy was a "Jesus Freak" in college. I didn't particularly like being around her. After all, I was a good Catholic and religiously attended Mass every Sunday; I just didn't want to hear all about Jesus and the Second Coming. It sort of scared me because I didn't know if I'd be ready or not if he did come back. A year after college graduation, I was living at home when Nancy asked if I knew anyone she could share an apartment with in Louisville, where she had just gotten a job. Wanting to move out of my parents' home, suddenly I heard myself saying, "Why don't we room together?"

Thinking better of my offer, I prefaced our move with the admonition, "Listen, Nancy, I'm a good Catholic and I know how you feel about Jesus. You believe what you want to believe and let me believe what I want to believe."

We shared an apartment together for two years. In that time I would see her daily reading her Bible and I knew she was praying for me. Periodically she would invite me to go to her inter-denominational church, New Covenant, with her. I always declined. Then one day she encouraged me to come with her with the words, "You'll meet some cute guys there!" That was all the bait I needed.

Next thing I knew, I was sitting in the middle of an auditorium filled with hand-clapping, arm-raising, tongue-speaking kids my age that seemed to have a warmth and sense of fellowship I had never experienced. I still couldn't wait to get out of there. Yet when the minister began to speak, it seemed that his words were directed right at me. Suddenly, I didn't want to leave. I wanted to have what all those people around me had.

I approached Nancy, and she and another friend, Mike, told me I needed to confess my sins to God. (That part wasn't hard. I'd grown up in a strict Catholic grade school in the '60s!) Then they laid hands on me, and we prayed for me to receive Jesus as my Lord and Savior and to be filled with the Holy Spirit. Then they encouraged me to pray. I began only as I knew how, "Our Father, who art in heaven . . . Hail Mary, full of grace . . ." I began reading the Gospel of John, and it was as if the words jumped off the page and spoke personally to me. Shortly after that as I drove to work, I was singing the new praise choruses I had learned, when the Lord blessed me with the gift of tongues.

My relationship with Jesus has changed my life. Though my motivation for attending New Covenant was not the best, the Lord used Nancy, Mike and New Covenant to move me closer to him. Now, twenty-two years later, I am married to a Methodist minister and we are both committed to serving the Lord and Savior I met so many years ago.

Night Light

Marjorie Qualls
Brookston

This seems so unreal, but it really restored my faith that there really is a God.

My Aunt Goldia, whom I felt was like a second mother to me, as she had no children of her own, seemed to take to my brothers and me.

She became very sick in a nursing home and was taken to a hospital and later moved to a care center. She was there for seven weeks. I visited her every day and even stayed all night for three nights. All the nurses marveled at her holding on so long.

She was ready to go but for one reason—God wasn't ready for her yet. She lay and prayed over and over "Dear Lord, please take me home," day after day. "Dear Jesus, please forgive me and take me in."

Then on Christmas Eve she saw a bright light. When I went the next day, she said to me, "I saw the light last night . . . it was so bright." She'd always been very alert, but I thought maybe she was kind of incoherent then. The rest of the day she was herself.

That night, she passed away as my great-granddaughter was working there in nurses training. I know the following to be true. The lady that was her roommate said that about midnight she awoke with such a bright light, it scared her. It was but a few seconds and then dark. Next morning she heard that Goldia had passed on.

I'm sure the Lord had come to take her with him and shined his light on her.

Night Messenger

Evelyn Kovachevich
South Bend

As I sit here today, on the anniversary of my beloved husband's death, I write this in his memory. He had a stroke in 1980 that put him in the hospital in a state of a blank mind due to the lack of oxygen to the brain, because the doctor forgot to order oxygen on his admittance.

After four months they told me he would be this way for the rest of his life. They were going to put him in a veterans' hospital or a nursing home. Oh God, he is only sixty-two and we were just now enjoying life and retirement together. He loved his home and family, travels to the West Coast to visit our son, a grandson, a grand-daughter—and he loved life itself. I prayed, "Please don't take him away from us. We worked together, played together, loved together, did everything together as one." I prayed, "Dear God, don't do this to us. Please God, not yet. . . ."

I was always careful to lock the doors at night, and make sure I was safe by myself. I went to bed with his absence on my mind and what I was going to do if they put him in another hospital and away from me. As I lay in bed, praying, thinking, trying to get some answers from somewhere, I heard a noise like a door opening. I could hear a movement like someone coming up the steps. I thought, "Oh my God, I forgot to lock the door and someone came in. Lay still, don't say a thing." It came closer and into the room, and I thought "I'm going to be raped or killed. Just be quiet and lay still."

I always lie on my stomach and could see by the side of me a bright illumined figure. I could not make out the figure, but it was a bright lighted figure, beautiful. All at once I felt a huge hand placed upon my right side, and a voice said "It is going to be all right. It's going to be all right." And the figure vanished like a snap of the finger. Next morning I got a call from my son who said to fire the doctor, and a new doctor would see Dad the next morn.

A new doctor did see him and they called me three days later to come and get my husband to take him home. We lived a happy fourteen years after this. Alex passed away on May 22, 1994, after seeing the tunnel of light and explaining to me how bright a light he had seen. He passed asking me for a kiss, a small love pat, and he died a very peaceful death. I can only thank God for this peace; he didn't pass away with pain. Thank you, God, for all your blessings you gave us.

With Open Arms

Theresa S. Phillips
Brownsburg

As I came home from the doctor, I received a call saying my aunt had had a brain hemorrhage, was in a coma and not expected to live through the night. We hurried to the hospital.

Mom and I stepped into my aunt's room. The only sound of life was the rushing of air into her oxygen mask. My cousin updated us saying my aunt was not responding and could not hear or see anything. Then she stepped out of the room.

With my aunt's eyes wide open and her head bent upwards and sideways, we leaned down by her face. We each took her hand and we told her how very much we loved her. I could see and feel her suffering. I told her, "Aunt Sondra, it is okay to let go. You do not have to fight any longer." Suddenly, she moved her eyes. I was moved to close my eyes and pray.

"Our father in heaven . . .," I prayed.

What happened next was something I never could have imagined. I saw a light enter the room. It was so bright and so brilliant, and luminous rays broke forth out of the light. As it drew closer I could see Jesus Christ, his brilliance indescribable—the feeling of presence, of warmth, of love no greater, of peace, of pureness no purer, of holiness no holier, of total divinity and infinite glory, of gentleness no gentler, of the strength in this Godly presence.

"Hallowed be thy name. . . ."

He slowly began to open up his arms as I continued to pray.

"For thine is the kingdom, and the power, and the glory . . . ."

His lips formed the words, "Come to me, my child."

I continued praying, "Oh Heavenly Father, please accept Aunt Sondra into your kingdom." I paused. "Aunt Sondra, Jesus is here. His arms are reaching for you. It's okay to go to Jesus. Please go to Jesus."

As I said, "Amen," I opened my eyes just as my aunt was ever so gently closing hers, and one solitary tear rolled down her face. Total and complete peace encompassed her lifeless body.

My mother started screaming, "My God, Theresa, she's gone. She's gone."

"I know," I said, "She went to God."

In the week that followed, I began to wonder about the experience. I prayed, "Lord, am I crazy? Was this experience really real?" I prayed over and over again, "Lord, please give me a sign. Please tell me what it is I am to do with this."

On Valentine's Day, I was on the phone talking with my dad about my experience when I heard the doorbell ring. It rang as if a young child was pushing it over and over and over again. My five-year-old son jumped up on the couch, with the doorbell still ringing, looked out the window and said, "Mommy, no one is here." As I looked onto our front porch, indeed, no one was there.

Was this my sign?

Now visions and signs are not a normal part of my life. I am startled and amazed about all of this. But, what I do know is—God has changed my life!

I know that God is so real, so alive, and continually offering his kingdom to each one of us. I now realize when Jesus opened up his arms it was not just for my aunt, it was for each of us.

I can honestly say, I have seen Jesus Christ. He is so beautiful, so sacred, and so very, very holy. And he is very much alive!

I want to shout with every ounce of my being, Praise God! Praise God! Praise God! He loves us with an incalculable love. His warmth is so great it fills every part of our being. His peace is so infinite that we are given unbelievable and total inner peace. And most important—we are to share his miracles with others.

Summer of Separation

Neil C. McGuffog
Indianapolis

It was summer time and the living was supposed to be easy. Unfortunately, this particular point in time marked my second month of being separated from my wife of six and a half years and our two small children, a twenty-month-old girl and a four-year-old boy. The anger, self-pity and resentment I felt over this episode in my life was sometimes overwhelming.

Thankfully, my estranged wife and I made a solemn commitment to focus on the children's best interests and to not make either child feel a part of this emotionally charged situation. The separation would lead to a quick divorce. That was the fall of 1995, and a lot of positive changes have happened in my life since. I wouldn't be able to say that if it were not for the complete willingness to turn my will and my life over to God, to accept life on life's terms, to practice some humility, and to be grateful.

The gratitude part brings me back to June 1995, the first summer after the separation. It was an incredibly difficult time for all of us. For me, I was trying to accept what God's will was for me. The pain of being separated from the children was most devastating. In my mind I projected both kids growing up as juvenile delinquents from a broken home. I felt a failure as a husband and a father and wondered how it would affect the kids long term. But mostly I was feeling self-pity.

It was a Sunday during that month of June and time for me to bring the children back to their mother's home after we'd spent a delightful weekend together. The weather was beautiful, and it was starting to cool down a bit as I helped them out of the car. They scurried into the garage eager to get inside to see their mom.

An incredible sadness overcame me. I didn't even bring their overnight bags inside the house. I dropped them at the threshold of the garage, called out to them good-bye, and got back in my vehicle. Intense anger and resentment filled my heart as I hoped I wouldn't see their mother before I could drive off.

As I backed down the driveway, I turned to look towards the garage where I saw the image of my precious twenty-one-month-old daughter. Standing there with reddish cheeks from the sun that weekend and her curls bouncing in the breeze, she was waving good-bye. I gave a cursory wave back and turned on to the road that I could hardly see because of the flood of tears. That image of my little precious daughter waving one of the many hundreds of good-byes she'll wave to her daddy and mommy was more than I could handle.

Miraculously, thank God, I had a thought: at least God gave her two strong legs to stand on as she waves. She's healthy and, if I have true faith, trust, and belief, God will take care of her and her brother during this most difficult time and throughout their lives.

Like the rain coming to an abrupt end after an intense summer downpour, the despair left me and a light feeling wrapped around my body. It's hard to describe the sensation. Gone was the anger, the self-pity, the resentment and the feeling that my kids were doomed. It was replaced with the most incredible feeling of gratitude for God's love that I have ever experienced. I often thank God for this episode, especially if I'm feeling sad.

The Right Child

Rebecca Smith
Mishawaka

All the women I knew, it seemed, were living life like the book—dating, falling in love, marrying, and becoming mothers. My twenties and thirties had come and gone. The decade of my forties was here and was passing by without a hint of a fulfilled dream. I only wanted what seemed normal.

Throughout the years I sought counseling and fought depression. The haunting question, "What purpose could you possibly have,

Lord, for not providing me with a spouse and family to witness to and experience the greatest gift of life?" jabbed my consciousness almost daily.

Besides a challenging career, I had submerged myself in travel, organizational responsibilities and small mission projects.

Still, in the back of my mind, I clung to a thread of hope. I could hang on a little longer waiting for a husband. I knew many beautiful marriages happened in midlife. The fading hope of motherhood, however, was almost more than I could accept. I was born with hip dysplasia which would make it hard to carry a child, and my biological clock was racing. At forty-two I felt it a bit late to consider children when there was no hint of a mate, and modern means of conception were out of the question. The door seemed locked.

I had spent the previous two summers as a volunteer in Romania hoping to give some happiness to the victims of Ceaucescu's regime—the orphaned children. Both summers were full of challenge and heartache, but were never considered a stepping stone for personal gain. I went, I worked and I returned home.

On my return home after the second trip, I had a significant dream where I was in a hospital bed (I don't know if it was a maternity or a psych ward), and my sister walked in holding a small child's hand. She indicated that this was now my child. I felt I was getting a strong poke in the ribs from God.

I made contact with a local adoption agency and soon my home study was completed and my application sent to World Association for Children and Parents (WACAP) in Seattle, Washington.

One little girl in my village orphanage of Tigveni particularly tugged at my heart. Although the Romanian teachers and staff tried to discourage me because of Vicuta's low mental ability, from September until March I pursued her as a prospective adoptee. I refused to believe she was retarded. When I received a detailed letter and sample of her writing skills, I knew as a single parent and after teaching all day, I would be faced with more than I could handle. I made a painful call to the agency to halt proceedings on Vicuta.

Within days, WACAP called with a lead of a much younger child of normal intelligence but physically handicapped. I was sent photos, videos and documents to examine. Physical ailments of my own to consider, the high risk of life-threatening disease in Romanian children to evaluate and the dim prognosis of her ever walking caused me to take another week to answer.

The challenge was great but I never lost a night's sleep. God's voice and hand were a part of my decision. There seemed to be no question that this was the right child for me. One of her ailments was something I've dealt with. I knew my parents had sacrificed for me, and it only seemed natural that I would provide for someone else.

From April to October I completed documents, faxed, phoned, wrote and prepared every last detail. On October 12, 1993, the door of the orphanage playroom was opened and my eyes and heart immediately spotted Aurelia, my new daughter, on the floor with outstretched arms. A caregiver reached down and placed a wet, dirty, but beautiful little girl with "Mama" on her lips into my arms. The dam broke and all feelings of love, gratitude and hope came pouring out.

My life has changed considerably since that day, but never has there been a hint of regret. The phone rings from various locations, and letters arrive from around the world asking about Aurelia.

Although my goal is to be the best Christian mother I have begged to be all these years, I also consider it my mission to share my story and provide support and assistance to prospective adoptive parents. I hope to convey to people the truth that things do work for good to those who love God. Perhaps we are called sometimes to make our dreams happen, and just maybe we have to come in the back door when the front one appears locked.

The Seventh Wave

Donald E. Foust
Kokomo

Once upon a time in 1985 I found myself chest deep in salt water. We were on the Hawaiian Island of Maui at the Kaanapali Hotel beach. There were three-foot waves that would lift you up and drop you down repeatedly. Once in a while a big one would come in and lift you up six or seven feet and drop you down ten feet on the back side.

I really enjoyed these waves but I soon noticed there were six waves three-feet high and the seventh was a big one. Surfers call this the seventh wave. It's the one they paddle out to and ride their surfboards on all the way back into the sandy beach. I couldn't figure out why there were always six and then the big seventh. Was it the wind? The currents? The gravity pulling on the water? I didn't know.

I began to think about all the sevens in the Bible. Seven days of creation, seven churches Paul wrote to, seven candles in the candelabra, the seven years after which all debts were forgiven and tithes were to be brought in. Seven seals in Revelation.

I just concluded God was causing the waves somehow through his laws of nature. Somehow he was causing two waves to occur at the same time to form the big seventh.

I enjoyed the waves for maybe an hour, and when I came out and stood on the shore, I noticed the six waves always came up the sand to the same mark. I found I could write in the sand just above the water line, "All My Sins" and then the seventh wave would follow and wipe away "All My Sins." It would do this over and over.

That's why we go to church, I believe. We worship together and say the Lord's Prayer and say "forgive us our trespasses" or debts or sins, and God does forgive them and gives us a clean start on a new week. Just like the seventh wave, he cleans our slate to start all over and do better.

Maybe the next time you say the Lord's Prayer you will remember the seventh wave and know he has wiped away all your sins for a new start.

Unexpected Calls

Pat Reiff
Warsaw

Everything that happens, good or bad, is for a reason. It prepares us for the future. On May 8, 1975, I was attending a home group Bible study. Our minister at the time, Rev. Chester, stopped the discussion and said, "We must go to prayer immediately and pray for Pat's family." I was shocked because my family was just fine; in fact, it had been a perfect day. Ralph, our youngest son, had been elected president of his high school's student body for the second year in a row. What or who could our minister be referring to? As soon as we finished prayer, he dismissed us and told us all to return to our homes.

At home I found police all around stopping every car on the road. Our truck was parked haphazardly in the yard with two bullet holes in the windshield—one exactly where the driver sits. When I parked our car, Ralph came running out of the house to assure me he was all right.

If we hadn't had a very obedient and faithful minister, I probably would have lost my son that night. Ever since then my testimony has been to tell others: if a name or memory becomes very strong in your mind, pray for them. We may never know why, but it's important. Twenty years later I found myself in another life-saving situation of a different kind.

On Sunday, February 26, 1995, I awoke at 5:00 A.M. with a voice telling me to pray for Ken Vance and his family who were missionaries in Zaire. I immediately got up and prayed for them. At worship service in church I asked for prayer for all our missionaries, but especially to remember the Ken Vance family. At 11:00 A.M. we went to prayer.

In May our church received a letter from Ken Vance telling us his wife, Debbie, had been bitten by a very poisonous snake, a puff adder, and about the terrible ordeal they went through. This happened at precisely the time we were in our 11:00 prayer at worship! No doctor was in the area. They used a snake vaccine on hand but found out the next day it was useless on puff adder bites. Normally, anyone bitten by a puff adder is dead within thirty minutes without the proper vaccine. But this didn't happen. She was very ill, she was numb to her waist, but she lived! When I read the letter, I started to cry with joyful tears and praised God for sending his angel to inform me of the Vances' need of prayer. Today, she is still very much alive and well!

I read the letter to my husband who said I should call our minister at that time, Chris. I told her I must write to the Vances and let them know what happened on this side of the world. It's so seldom we ever know why we get these strange messages. When I found out Debbie lived, I was overjoyed to think my obedience helped save her life. Because my son's life was spared through Rev. Chester's obedience and faithfulness, he prepared the way for me to obey when I was asked. The best part was, I just knew it was all our prayers that did it!

It is so humbling to think I was chosen to pray for them and He heard my prayers, along with our faithful congregation at Morris Chapel U.M.C. Thanks be to God I did not forget what he did for me and mine twenty years ago.

What Matters

Sue Atkinson
Garrett

At the time of my severe wreck in June, 1993, I already truly believed God loved me and was always close to me. That day my faith was raised to a completely new level. It was reported by one local TV station that I had been killed in the wreck. That was almost true. My blood pressure went to zero four different times before arriving at the hospital by helicopter. One ankle was severely fractured as well as several ribs and my sternum. A head injury caused one eye to be crossed.

As I awoke in the Intensive Care Unit, I saw bags of fluids and blood entering my body and thought "Am I going to live or die?" Instantly a masculine voice in my head replied, "It doesn't matter! God is with you here, God will be with you there!" Almost immediately I fell asleep. When I woke, my reaction was "Wow!"

Since then, there have been nine surgeries on my ankle and one on my eye. It has not been a smooth road. In numberless ways, God has shown his love for me as an individual, just as I am. When my clock chimes the quarter hour I hear "In Times Like These." If I forget to pick up the telephone from the bathroom cabinet, within minutes the thought of going after something in the bedroom occurs to me. On the way by, I see the phone and retrieve it. These coincidences happen several times each day. Through my devotions and Bible study classes, I am guided and directed daily. The words and thoughts expressed in theses studies apply to my life personally. I'll probably never under-stand how the biblical writers and others could write something years ago that exactly speaks to me on the very day I need it!

What a difference in my life! My body still gives me a lot of pain, and I'll always walk with quite a limp. It's well worth it! I wouldn't recommend it to anyone else as a way to grow, but God has lifted me from the level of believing in him, to the complete knowledge that he loves me. There is no comparison with my former life. Now when I feel a nudge to do something, I don't just dismiss the feeling and go on with what I am doing — I do what I'm urged to do. Sometimes the nudge is to go to the store right then instead of a couple hours later. Almost without fail there is someone who needs to talk and who will open up to me. Other times there may be no visible result, but later the puzzle all fits together. It happens much too often to be logical or circumstantial. It comes from being led by God to touch someone else's life. I pray I will always be sensitive to these nudges, and I urge others to respond to their nudges. The positive feedback is fantastic.

There was no tunnel of light, no visible angel, but the life-changing words, "It doesn't matter," will never leave my memory. What a voyage this has been! God is still using me even though I'm very slow-moving, sometimes very forgetful and have very little strength. I am so grateful I can be of use to him and to others. Most of all, though, I am thankful to know that he loves me. No doubt about it. God is good, all the time. All the time, God is good!

Part Two

PRAYER, ANSWERED AND OTHERWISE

After Forty Years, a Prayer

Michael T. Boardman
Waynetown

I was a typical guy, the only time I would go to the doctor was at the emergency room for stitches or something like that. I had not seen a family physician since the early 1970s, prior to this.

In the fall of 1993, I developed a skin problem because of being exposed to Agent Orange some twenty-five years earlier. As a part of the usual procedure at the doctor's office, they check blood pressure. Mine was so high that, on top of medicine for the skin problem, I was told I needed an anti-hypertensive.

For two years the blood pressure medicine controlled the problem, then my blood pressure began to go back up. My doctor changed my medicine about once a month, until he referred me to a specialist who, after numerous, often painful procedures, diagnosed me with a 90 percent blockage in the artery to my left kidney.

I was informed that surgery was the only effective way to save the kidney and control my blood pressure, before I had a stroke or heart attack. To say I was scared was a real understatement.

I was always in control of everything that had happened all my life up until now. After a few days of worry, I felt that I was no longer in control of this part of my life; so, for the first time in about forty years I asked God for something. I asked him to take charge of my life. I did not expect any reply, because I hadn't lived my life any way close to what I know, now, that God wants. However, my prayers were answered immediately. I felt like a huge weight had been lifted from my shoulders, and that God would see that everything would work out fine.

As it turned out, even though I did not know it at the time, I was on a prayer chain in Florida, Michigan, and at least two in Indiana.

I was referred to a vascular surgeon, who decided to try angioplasty (balloon) surgery first before surgery to replace the artery. The angioplasty worked, at least enough to avoid replacement surgery.

When I came home from the hospital, I had an uncontrollable urge to start reading the Bible, which I had not done since Vacation Bible School. The urge was so strong that I read the Bible almost daily. My wife, who has been a Christian since she was twelve years old, could not believe the change in me after my surgery.

I continued to read the Bible and started attending church regularly after a few months. In October 1996, at the age of forty-eight, I accepted the Lord Jesus Christ as my personal savior and was baptized.

Later, I called my brother who lives about fifty miles away and told him I had accepted Christ into my life. He then checked his prayer journal and, unbeknownst to me, he and his wife had put a request in at their church for a prayer that I accept Christ. It was dated one month before I had been baptized.

God does answer our prayers, even the ones of a sinner like me.

Chewing Up Anger

Marilyn Griffith
New Albany

When I remember the God events in my life, I am drawn to an annual conference many years ago. We were camping at Raynetown and commuting each morning to the conference sessions. My heart was heavy with hurt and anger toward a clergy member who had been unkind to my husband. Twenty six years later, I can still say the clergy person was unkind and caused unnecessary pain over a period of time.

Late at night, I sat on the picnic table under the stars and begged, "God, I need your help with my anger. It's chewing me up," At 1:00 A.M. with no relief, I turned in.

At 10:00 A.M. the next morning, Rev. Loren walked up to me and said, "Marilyn, I'd like to take you to lunch in the Tudor Room. You need to talk." Although I had known Loren in college, we had never spent time alone in conversation with each other. Furthermore, asking someone else's spouse to lunch was not something Loren or I would do in those days. I had never shared with him the intensity of my concern, but he knew exactly what needed to be healed. He listened and nurtured, and by the time we had polished off the chocolate covered pecan balls, I was at peace.

When I reflect on Paul's mediation between Philemon and Onesimus, I am reminded and humbled by the time God answered my prayer through his servant, Loren, and I am grateful.

In God's Time

Lisa Whittaker
Valparaiso

As a teenager, I was always self conscious about my weight and looks. When I reached college, I can remember wishing that I had some health problem that would make me thin, but not kill me. Let's face it, I was obsessed! In 1987, in my first year of marriage, my wish came true; I was diagnosed with Crohn's Disease. I had my rapid weight loss; but what came with the weight loss, I wasn't prepared for and didn't want.

The first couple of years with this disease were very tough; going from one medicine to the next, the abdominal pain, the inconvenience, the humiliation of this disease and its symptoms were just too much. I turned to God, praying for him to heal my body, but time and again, no answer seemed to come. After the birth of my first child, Taylor, this disease really began to anger me. There were mornings when my daughter would be crying in her crib for me to come get her, but I couldn't because the symptoms of this disease held me hostage in my bathroom. Soon, my anger turned to God for not hearing my prayers and not doing what I asked him to do. How could he just turn his back on me?

In 1993, my family moved to northwest Indiana, and with the stress of moving came a flare-up with this ugly disease. With the flare-up came the straw that broke the camel's back. I felt abandoned by God, so I was going to abandon him as well. Little did I know, great things were about to happen to me—all compliments of God. With a new doctor and new medicine, my Crohn's was brought under control, and we found a new church. I was still a bit hesitant about my faith, but then God led me to a ladies' Bible study in this new church, and my faith and knowledge began to flourish.

With the birth of our twin sons, Aaron and Ethan, and all the problems we went through the first year with them as premature infants, the lesson of a lifetime also surfaced. This lesson was that I had to learn to wholeheartedly put my trust in God no matter what the outcome; I had to accept that God is in charge and not me. This was easier said than done, especially when dealing with the life of your own children.

However, I did learn it all too well, and a year after their birth, I began to pray again for healing from this Crohn's disease; but again, no answer seemed to come. I had begun to accept that God's answer was "no" and that for whatever purpose, he was going to use this disease in me for some good. On May 4, 1997, that good was about to come to light. I went to the emergency room because of some abdominal pain that I had been having for four days. They admitted me and my doctor thought it was my Crohn's again, though I kept telling him that the pain was different.

On May 6, he scheduled a colonoscopy to see what was going on, and fifteen minutes before the surgery was to start, I began to pray. It was odd that this feeling began to wash over me and my thoughts turned to "Lord, let's show these people what a miracle looks like, and I will tell everyone I can what a blessing you gave me." As soon as I said that, my pastor walked in and read a scripture from Psalms and in it, it said "I will heal all your diseases" and with that, I knew great things were about to happen.

Sure enough, when the procedure was over, in much surprise, my doctor said, "Your Crohn's is gone." I was still a little groggy from the anesthesia, so I had to ask him to repeat it a few times, but in my heart I knew it was true. After ten years of struggling, learning, and praying, God's answer finally came, but it was in his time, not mine; he was in charge, not me.

Mountain Dreams

Julie Gilleand
Mishawaka

Single-parenting three boys, managing the household, and working part-time for so many years had left me depleted of energy and the willpower some days to even get out of bed, dreading the onslaught of daily pressures. I wished I could quit my job so there would be more time to keep up with housework, and so I'd not be tired and grumpy for my kids in the evening. But not having much choice in the matter, I wondered if maybe the Lord would at least make a way for me to have a little vacation. It was, after all, a need; and the Bible says that ". . . my God shall supply all my need." So, I began to pray about it.

Just for fun, I began dreaming of where I would like to go if given a choice. Colorado! (I was really dreaming big.) I didn't seriously expect God to provide that big of a trip. A weekend at a local hotel would even be a nice break. But it was fun to dream . . . towering mountains, soaring eagles, the scent of spruce trees filling the air, scattered wildflowers and the orange, pink, and purple western sky at sunset. Yes! This is where I would go if only I could. Being close to nature, I thought, would fill me with the serenity I so needed. The noise, busyness and stress which filled my days felt like voices screaming at me from every angle. My heart, itself, was screaming for peace.

Although I made the desires of my heart known to God, I left everything up to him. He knew what was best for me, and however he chose to provide, I knew would be perfect. Even so, my longing for the West and the mountains continued to grow. It was an idea I just couldn't shake.

At work one day in the church office, I was running the Sunday bulletins through the folding machine when the picture on the cover caught my eye. A lush, green, mountain valley with mountains towering above, shining golden-red in the sunlight. At the base of the mountains lay a lake so still you could see in it a perfect reflection of the peaks above. Breathtaking! "Oh Lord, what would it be like to stand in this very spot and see with my own eyes this awesome display of Your beautiful artwork," I prayed.

Weeks passed and many prayers were prayed, as what had started as a simple thought was fast developing into a dream. Most of my friends thought I was setting up for a big disappointment. But more and more I felt that this idea was not just mine, that it was God who had planted it in my heart.

The main obstacle was money. Even a weekend trip would cost more than I had. Yet I believed that if this was God's will, he'd make a way. No matter how skinny my billfold, God "owns the cattle on a thousand hills."

A few weeks later, I received a gift in the exact amount of money needed to pay for my trip, from a very unexpected source. God had wonderfully provided.

The trip was everything I dreamed of and more. Looking out my hotel window at the wondrous mountains all around, I spotted a cross on top of the highest peak. I felt the Lord saying to me, "Here are the mountains and rest you so longed for. I am with you and it is I who brought you here. It is my gift to you." Praise the Lord for this special blessing.

The Maroon Bells near Aspen was the special mountain spot on the cover of the church bulletin. Though I did catch a glimpse of it from a distance, it was not until my second trip to Colorado a year later, that I was able to stand on the bank of Maroon Lake together with my three boys and gaze upon the awesome wonder of God's creation. It was an emotional moment as I remembered praying over the picture of this very spot, longing to be there.

What I have learned is that not only does God care about our dreams, but often it is he who has planted them in our hearts. And if, indeed, he is the giver of the dream, he is well able to provide a way.

One Kind of Genuine Miracle

Lynne DeMichele
Indianapolis

It's been many years since I first heard that terrifying diagnosis and long past time giving credit publicly where credit's due.

One morning I woke up in pain with what felt like a severe cramp in the left side of my face. When I looked in the mirror, a gargoyle stared back at me. Mardy, my husband, and I both thought it must have been some sort of stroke that left my face so suddenly and radically disfigured. Later that morning our family doctor scratched his head and referred me to a neurologist.

When I heard the words "multiple sclerosis" for the first time, a wave of incredulity and panic swept over me. During the days waiting for results from the spinal tap and a string of other tests, we tried to remain confident. But my symptoms were exacerbating; my whole body seemed to be in some kind of revolt. Images of helpless invalids and pitying friends kept intruding on my thoughts. Mardy, never betraying a hint of worry, said "We're in this together. Whatever it is, we'll handle it together."

The diagnosis was confirmed. I felt like I'd been dropped on some hostile, alien planet. But I was gratefully aware that I wasn't there alone.

A temporary medical leave at work allowed me to concentrate on healing. It also allowed me to sink into a slough of self-pity and anxiety. Where would the money come from for the enormous medical costs? How would my relationship with my sons, my friends, my husband change? Who would care for me—or them—when it got even worse?

Then the calls started. "We're praying for you," they said, "We've got you on our prayer chain." "We're keeping you surrounded with loving, healing thought." Increasingly, I felt lifted on a rising current of positive energy. The best of it was I didn't feel pitied—only loved. It was especially therapeutic being able to laugh about some of the odd accommodations those around me provided. One day when my legs suddenly refused to work, my youngest son lent me his skateboard so I could get around the house until a more dignified conveyance could be gotten.

After an astonishingly short period of time, I found myself recovering lost faculties. My mother, whose prayers I always suspected got to God first, proclaimed it a genuine miracle.

Multiple sclerosis is known as an incurable disease. It may leave you alone for awhile but it always comes back. And while it continues to ambush me from time to time, I know my mother was right. It was a genuine miracle. My body wasn't cured in any literal sense, but my soul has been renewed. I'm no longer afraid of what will happen; the dread and self-pity are all gone.

I don't have the right words for it. I just know that what I understand as grace has a great deal to do with it. I know I am unconditionally loved and never alone. And all that is surely a miracle of a most amazing kind.

Praying for Parents

Barbara Hayes Howell
Noblesville

My parents died when I was young, and I lived with my grandmother for a while. When she became infirm, I went to live with a half-sister and her family who lived in the country. It was at this time that I took Jesus as my personal savior and asked him to direct my paths. During my teenage years I often prayed that God would someday lead me to a husband who would have loving parents whom I could look on as my parents, too.

Just prior to high school graduation, I was offered a job as secretary in a law firm in a nearby town. I readily accepted the job and found a small place of my own. Shortly thereafter, my best friend, Ruth Ann, contacted me and said she was taking a job at the local telephone company and would be living with her aunt and uncle. She asked if I would like to share a room with her at their house. This sounded ideal. We'd always had such fun together, and I had met "Aunt Martha and Uncle Lisle" and liked them. So, the move was made.

Aunt Martha and Uncle Lisle loved having giggling girls around and joined in our fun. Having no children of their own, they embraced us fully. When Ruth Ann announced that she and her high school boyfriend planned to marry in the fall, I began to think about my future. One day Aunt Martha and Uncle Lisle said they'd like to talk with me. They had applied at an adoption agency, but had never had a child placed with them. They said they wanted children of their own and wanted to adopt me; and would I want to adopt them? What a wonderful surprise! God really worked wonders and in a way I never dreamed of. I had a family of my own, now! I talked with my law firm about the adoption and they thought it was great. In fact they handled it, and I typed my own adoption papers!

While singing in our church choir, I met and eventually married Dick. He did have wonderful Christian parents whom I came to love very much. My parents have since gone to be with God, but they were a very important part of our lives; and we know that God worked in a wonderful way to answer our prayers. I not only got the in-laws I'd prayed for, but—as God so often does—he gave me more than I asked for.

Strong Medicine

Jay Sommers
Greentown

I was at work in June 1969 when I had a terrible pain in my lower back. I left work and went home, then on to our family doctor, who gave me a shot for pain and sent me to the hospital. They were unable to find the cause, and after a couple of days they did exploratory surgery. The surgeon who operated said I had a tumor the size of a volleyball but because of where it was attached he could not remove it. He told me he would send me about sixty miles to Methodist Hospital in Indianapolis where they would give me cobalt treatments and melt it away like a dish of ice cream. Cobalt was about the only treatment for cancer at the time. I found out later that my family doctor told my mother that I would not live out the year.

Methodist Hospital set up forty-eight cobalt treatments. I took five treatments a week, and I was glad for the break over the weekend. When the series of treatments was over I thought I was cured. However, the terrible pain came back the next June. This time I could get cobalt near home, so the doctor said he would give me stronger treatments along with medicine to keep me from getting sick. He set up thiry-two treatments. After the treatments the tumor was still there. He said the cobalt would continue to work for a couple of weeks. At that time he scheduled ten more treatments. I had a wife and three small children—one, a very headstrong boy. The time when I was all alone in the treatment room became very strong prayer time. I also had a lot of friends and many churches praying for me.

By the time these ten treatments were over, I had a cobalt burn on my back and my wife was to rub a special lotion on it. Two weeks later X-rays were taken and the doctor said the tumor was still there, but he knew of nothing else that could be done. It was now up to a higher power.

That was almost twenty-seven years ago. I have no cancer, just problems from too much cobalt. I now thank the Lord for the cancer, because it brought my family closer to God. Each of my three children and their spouses love the Lord and are active in the church. They are also bringing up their children to love the Lord. Praise God!

Stubborn Streak

Donita Hiatt
Westfield

There I was again sitting on the edge of the bed, praying as I had for many years—inserting the same sentence as always, "Lord, please take this stubborn streak that I have been cursed with, so I can be a better servant."

My mother had told me all the years I was growing up that "You are so stubborn, I can't do anything with you," and "You are the most stubborn child in the state of Indiana," and "I want to love you, but you are so mean and bullheaded nobody can love you." So, I thought of my bullheaded stubbornness as a curse that made me hard to love.

As usual I went to sleep soon after. But this night was different. About 1:00 A.M. I found myself wide awake. Memories were flooding my mind, things I hadn't remembered up to this point, happenings that had been in my subconscious for many years.

At thirty-eight years of age, I was recalling many hurts and hardships in my life. Having grown up in an abusive, dysfunctional family, there were many things I didn't want to remember.

After about twenty minutes I said, "I am going to quit thinking about this stuff and go back to sleep." But sleep would not come. Instead, after three hours I decided to get up and write down what I was remembering and feeling as I recalled the "junk" of my life.

As I wrote, more and more of those memories flooded from my mind and I tried to record everything; when, after four hours, my mind finally went blank. I lay back in the lounge chair and fully relaxed and felt complete peace. I wasn't tired, but refreshed.

After about fifteen minutes, I picked up the papers and began to realize that I didn't understand what had happened or why these last few hours had transpired.

I started reading aloud the thirteen pages I had written. There were tears and shaking as memories of abuse and fighting became sharper in my mind. After reading it all, I began asking God, "Why did I have to go through all of this? What am I supposed to gain by reliving all the hurts of my childhood?"

The answer was there immediately. I heard, "Don't be afraid of your past. It was because of your stubbornness that you survived and grew. It was your stubbornness that I gave you that made you seek and find a better way and to reach for happiness. Without this determination you would not have been as strong as you were and you would still be carrying the scars. Don't ask to have your stubbornness and determination removed; instead, thank me for them and always use them for good and it will be a blessing to you."

Some have called me crazy. Others believed I had a wild imagination. But I know that I have gotten a direct message from God.

There have been many hardships since that night. Each one has been survived and I have been strengthened with each one, because I have learned to use what God has given me.

No longer do I consider stubbornness a curse. I have been greatly blessed.

Praise the Lord!

Miracle Girl

Timothy Watters
Fort Wayne

On July 9, 1996, my wife, Julie, gave birth to our first child — a fine, healthy boy we named Zachary. Mother and baby did well for the first few days after coming home, but then Julie began to feel ill. At first it was thought to be exhaustion, then flu, then an intestinal infection. But in spite of rest and medication, Julie's condition seemed to get worse.

On July 24, at 3:00 A.M., I rushed Julie to the hospital, while her mother stayed with Zach. Julie's condition rapidly deteriorated. She complained of a sensation of fluid in her abdomen, and was running a fever. Throughout the day, numerous tests were performed to try to determine what was making her ill. Finally, two gastroenterologists called our family together to tell us they had found that the tissue of Julie's large intestine was dying, and that an emergency operation was necessary to save her life.

Julie was taken to surgery at 9:30 that night, and at midnight the surgeon called us together to tell us that things had gone very well. He had had to perform an ileostomy and also had to remove about seventy percent of Julie's large intestine, because it was essentially dead; but that she appeared to be healthy, otherwise.

At about 7:00 the next morning, I returned to the hospital, expecting to talk to my wife and to tell her how much I loved her. As I approached her room in the Intensive Care Unit, however, a nurse stopped me and told me that during the night Julie had apparently suffered a stroke. Her left side was paralyzed, and she could no longer speak. Her brain was also swelling, which could be life threatening.

During the next few days, I prayed for Julie's healing and for strength to face the challenges ahead. At this time the doctors could not assure me that she would live, or what she would be like if she did live. I had to fact the possibility of raising our son alone. But even if there was no realistic hope of Julie's fully recovering, I trusted that God would make everything work to his glory and to accomplish his purpose. On three occasions, I was called to the hospital because Julie was near death. Each time, God brought her from the edge.

In order to give her brain a chance to heal, the neurologists had placed Julie in a drug-induced coma. About five weeks after being admitted to the hospital, the doctors decided to bring her out of the coma. They warned us not to hope too much, for they feared that Julie would not be functioning at a very high level.

Over the next few days, as the drug wore off, Julie began to open her eyes, then responded to questions with movements of her head, then to talk! She was moved to a rehabilitation ward where she began to walk again. Two weeks later, she was home. She now cares for Zach and me as though nothing ever happened.

Not long before being released from the hospital, a neurologist new to Julie's case came to examine her. He greeted her with, "So you're the Miracle Girl!" No one has said it better.

Waiting for Hope

Scott K. Stephans
Noblesville

We decided to wait to have children. Postponing that blessed event for two or three years seemed like good wisdom. The plan was first to enjoy building a solid relationship between the two of us. Then we would work on raising two or three kids. We never expected that we would have difficulty having children.

The first infertility specialist said the chances of us having our own child were slim. He recommended we try some things to improve those chances. Month after month we followed the doctor's prescribed routine. Still no pregnancy. The second infertility specialist said there was no chance. He concluded it would be impossible for us to have our own biological children. That discouraging word along with many more months of disappointment caused us to seriously question God's will for our lives.

Were we to live childless? Were we to adopt? We love children. One of us grew up with seven younger brothers and sisters. One of us is an elementary teacher. We adore our nieces and nephews and friends' children. We believe God placed a holy passion in our souls for children. To not have one of our own was the greatest heartache of our lives.

For thirteen years we tried with no success to have a baby. Finally we came to a point of surrender. It was time to give up the emotional struggle of the past one hundred and fifty months. It was time to give up our dream of a home with a mom and a dad and a few children. We thanked God for a fulfilling marriage and a wonderful life of Christian discipleship.

But God did not give up. One day, out of the blue, we received a healthcare newsletter in the mail. It contained a special feature article detailing a new treatment for infertility. Immediately we felt God renew our hope. With anxious reserve we went to talk to this specialist (the third one in ten years). He told us there was hope. As he explained our options, we felt a new and exciting assurance fill our hearts. God was preparing us for a miracle. After eight more months of discussion and prayer, we trusted the Lord to lead us through this new procedure.

In May we heard the best news of our life, "You're pregnant!" And, on the twelfth day of Christmas our true love gave us a precious little girl baby. What could we name her? What else—Hope.

What Adam Really Saw

Greg Rominger
New Palestine

"For God so loved the world that he gave his only son, that whoever believes in him shall not perish but have eternal life" (John 3:16). This verse really says it all, doesn't it? It is hard for me to imagine the kind of love that could go beyond the love we feel for our children.

I came to appreciate this even more last Lenten season, when we were faced with the possibility of losing our own son Adam. Adam was diagnosed with leukemia at the age of nineteen months. He went into remission, and his treatment seemed to be going well until last spring (about a year and a half after his diagnosis). After several bouts with infections, Adam had a routine blood test that made his doctor suspect a relapse. In Adam's case, a relapse would be a very grave situation.

At that point in my life I could not imagine the type of love God has for us, the kind that would allow him to willingly sacrifice his son; because, I would have done anything to save our child. But what could we do? Pray.

As fate would have it, we learned of the doctor's suspicions late on a Friday afternoon. Unfortunately the lab that could read the results of a bone marrow test was already closed for the weekend. The doctor assured us that waiting until Monday would not hurt Adam, so we would have to wait to find out. This didn't seem fair—why should we have to wait all that time? How could we stand not knowing for so long?

Beth started calling everyone we knew who was a Christian and asking them to pray for Adam and to put him on prayer chains at their churches. By Saturday morning, I can not even guess how many people were praying from Adam. Meanwhile he continued to feel horrible and so did we.

That afternoon when Adam took a nap, I decided to get some air by running an errand, so I took Rachel and left for a couple of hours. While we were gone, Adam woke from his nap and came out and laid down on the couch in our family room. As Beth watched him from across that silent room, a strange expression suddenly crossed his face. He looked at Beth, puzzled, and asked, "Why did those people say that?"

"What people? Say what, Adam?" Beth asked.

Adam looked at her in total disbelief that she had neither heard nor seen what he was talking about, and said, "Those people right there! Why did they say I was going to be all right?"

Had Adam just seen angels?

When Rachel and I returned a little while later, I found Adam up playing and obviously feeling the best he had in some time. As Beth related what had happened, she said, "Now for the first time in a long time, I think Adam is going to be all right."

We continued to pray (as did many others), and Adam continued to show improvement. When we went to the doctor's office for the bone marrow test, the expressions on the faces of the doctor and nurse betrayed their fears that they did not expect the news to be good.

The doctor drew the bone marrow, prepared the sample on a slide, and studied it under his microscope for several minutes. Finally he walked into the room, looked at us and said, "Have you been praying?" We quickly answered yes. Then he said, "because his test is negative, he hasn't relapsed." Thank God!

Thank you, God, for your incomprehensible love. For the love that gave us Jesus, the love that shows us mercy. And thank you, Lord, for allowing us to come to you in prayer. Help us to recognize and use the times in our lives when we have the opportunity to pray.

Part Three

UNEXPECTED ANGELS

Crowd of Angels

Pamela Keith
Columbus

It was July 19. The pain in my abdomen had returned, bringing seventeen hours of vomiting. By 5 A.M., July 20, I could hardly walk, was seeing double and very short of breath. In the emergency room they found a blood pressure of eighty-three over ten, severe dehydration and blood counts off the chart—pancreatitis.

I don't remember much about the rest of that day. When I woke up I was unable to talk. I learned that it was August 5. What had happened since July 20?

As the days went by I learned that I couldn't talk because they had put in a tracheal tube. My kidneys had failed, I had had almost daily dialysis, had respiratory arrest, and had been on a respirator all that time. Bill and our family had been told there was a 70 percent mortality rate with this pancreatitis, but because of my lifestyle, a 40 percent mortality rate—not the news they were expecting.

Those sixteen days had been very difficult for everyone. I didn't have the ability to pray or even try to understand what was going on. Mine was the easiest sixteen days, because I was unaware. But those who waited persevered with faith and prayer.

The community of faith—my local church and many others in churches throughout our city and several states—persevered on my

43

behalf. They maintained contact with Christ through prayer and meditation and contact with other Christians as they came together in
prayer. Prayer vigils took place at the hospital. People prayed at their
altars. The power of those prayers brought me back to life. Some of
those folk call me their miracle. But it's God's miracle, because of their
perseverance in prayer.

A Tough Nut to Crack

Jack Dwiggins
Brookston

I have often prayed for and thought that someday I would
tell my story of a transformation in my life similar to Saul's change to
Paul on the road to Damascus. At that high point I would become the
perfect loving, caring, forgiving, evangelistic and dynamic Christian
husband, father, friend, and disciple. Well that hasn't happened, and
over the years I suppose I have envied those whose stories were like
Paul's. But I have come to realize that God's way of moving me forward
has been different: slower, many ups and downs, saved and lost over
and over. It's possible that I am a really tough nut to crack.

I grew up in southern Indiana and my parents always went to
church. Our family first attended the Pleasant Hill United Methodist
Church and later the Geneva United Methodist Church, a two-point
charge, served by the same pastor. I am convinced that God wanted me
to find my faith through the lives of laypersons in those churches and
two others later in my life.

I did have my share of opportunities to be saved "all at once," for
we had several revivals during that time. Those experiences did not
change me immediately; but, I do believe they built up a reservoir of
feelings that kept me close to or near the church later in life. As youth
in the Geneva church we were served by a student pastor who would
dance with us, a retired Wesleyan pastor who forbid us to dance, and a
pastor who was a transfer from a fundamentalist church who wasn't

sure what he believed about dancing. Some might think that this range of emotions would have been harmful for that Methodist Youth Fellowship, but I believe it challenged us while we were searching for our faith. From that small group came a senior pastor of a church in northern Indiana, an individual who has an independent ministry in the Indianapolis area, persons who continue to be active in those churches, and the North Indiana Conference lay leader.

To me, the common thread for us was the mentoring we received from the faithful laypersons in those congregations. We were influenced by Sunday School teachers, saints like the older lady who would drive her buggy to church and constantly encourage all of the youth with her kindness and wisdom, and other leaders who would allow us to sing, preach, and participate fully in the life of the church. Two of us were lay speakers in our district at the ripe old age of seventeen.

I am convinced that for me, and probably for many others, the church is the only place where we can find the pieces that will sustain us as we strive to grow in faith and become the disciples Jesus has called us to be.

Now, for me, the important task is to become the mentor that provides the experiences for others so they may grow in faith. Some have suggested that I try to do too much in the church. Some may have said that to those lay persons at Geneva and Pleasant Hill. If so, I'm glad they didn't listen. They and many others gave me my life, including the pastors who prayed with me and for me and guided my spiritual journey.

Is it possible God wanted me to know the importance of lay witness so that I might be an effective lay leader for the conference? Certainly, Jesus gave me the model to follow. I must be in the business of changing people's lives in a positive way. My mentors over the years understood that call and responded. I praise God for their ministry.

Candles for a Dismal Soul

Dave Douglas
Indianapolis

Have you ever been at your wit's end, at the end of your rope, without hope of life ever getting back to a semitolerable place? I wasn't asking for much, I didn't want a perfect life, I just wanted to have a life that I could stand! I was at this point three years ago. From all outward indications I was a successful high-tech computer professional making a good wage, on the go and in the know, owning a perfect life, loving a perfect wife, living in a mansion up in Noblesville, flying to L.A. sometimes twice a year just to see the grandchildren, flying to Washington D.C., Boston, Phoenix and San Jose several times a year on business.

My children, wife, closest friends, coworkers, and customers—none of them—knew the miserable, real me inside the walls I had erected for privacy and protection. I was a chronic perfectionist and tormented with a constant drive to be more, be better in all that I did. I, therefore, suffered from acute inferiority and anxiety when I, more often than not, failed to meet my own self-imposed, unrealistic high standards.

Two years ago I had some kind of a mental starve-out or breakdown crisis where all of a sudden I was looking at the demise of my second, fifteen-year marriage—the one that I thought had been conceived in heaven. Nothing I tried would save it. Two of my children and I hadn't spoken for twelve years. My company was down the tubes; my retirement of thirty plus years had been mismanaged and seemed to have gone south without me getting to book a flight to go along. I had just lost a $15,000 investment in a couple of futures scams. I had a bitter stinging rash all over the upper half of my body, face and soul. I didn't have one thing in my life to be proud of or value. I was fifty years old and facing the downhill slide. In my pastor's words, "Life had given me too many boxes of manure to handle." At the time I wasn't an optimist, therefore I wasn't "looking for the pony in it."

One evening I found myself and my shotgun on the creek bank behind our home, stalking a pair of beavers that had set up a damn and were felling our prized young walnut trees for building materials. After about a week of much soul searching during the before-dawn and after-dusk vigils with no luck of any beaver sightings, I decided to just use the shotgun to put myself out of my misery. For some reason, after I had completely rationalized all the fear out of the prospect by weighing the advantages of taking one's life versus going through another painful divorce again—complete with the shame and anxiety of telling dear friends, neighbors, loved stepchildren, and in-laws goodbye; I decided coolly just not to. I think I had also asked for some kind of a sign to do it or not, and it never came. Today, I know the reason for my decision.

At that time of my blackest period, as far as I know now, there was only one person that knew of my anguish. A programmer with whom I had worked closely on several projects somehow had been able to peer into the walls of my darkened soul and was able to tell there was a lot of hurt and not much else in there. She didn't know what to do or say to me directly at the time, but later she told me that all during this period, each week when she would go to church, she would light a candle and say a prayer just for me. This is a married person with the responsibilities of her own beautiful family to take care of and nurture, and yet she cared enough about a lost, hurting, dismal soul inside a coworker to pray a special prayer for him—week-in and week-out.

I thank God for beautiful people like this precious one. She happens to be a Catholic, but I have and continue to meet more saints like her in my church home here at St. Luke's. I have never encountered such a wonderful feeling of God's unconditional love in such magnitude at any other church I have ever visited. I feel like the prodigal son that has finally come home. I know there have to be other wonderful church communities, therefore I pray daily for all of them, also. I have committed to pattern my life after this plan to help my fellow humans any and every way I can.

I started attending Saint Luke's Singles meetings sometime in March of 1996. At the same time I started attending services there. I would shed tears of remorse, repentance, gratitude and joy through all of the sermons, and even most of the musical parts of the worship (and still do). At times it was downright embarrassing, but it felt so good!

I didn't feel good about myself, however, until sometime in September of that year. It took much prayer, about four dozen self-help books, several divorce recovery workshops, several group programs, many gallons of both bitterly painful and wonderfully joyful tears, getting involved in church and choir activities, many hours of constructive conversations with friends, hundreds of hugs of encouragement.

And now, I could say that I feel like I have been born again, but that wouldn't be a powerful enough statement. It feels more like I am living now for the first time ever! My most often felt emotion is extreme gratitude for Grace.

Christ as a Bag Lady

Andrea Leininger
Brownsburg

Dear Madelin, You brought Jesus to me when you climbed aboard the plane in McClean, Virginia. You held him gently in your arms while riding in Corky's car on the way to the Abbey. You cared for him patiently and affectionately until I was ready to see him on Saturday morning. So lovely, he was, Madelin. His eyes sparkled. His smile was contagious. I think I loved him at first sight.

At 8 P.M. Sunday, you invited me into his room. We spent ninety minutes together talking. He looked so distressed when we talked about evil in the world. His appearance changed to sadness when we spoke of the death of loved ones. A kind of compassion filled that small room. Without quite knowing it was happening, he claimed my heart. I wanted to kneel and pray. I wanted to draw close and hug him, but it was too sacred a moment. For surely glory surrounded him and it was too great for me to touch! Yet, as I breathed in the air of the room, I realized my lungs were filling with the clean, fresh air of God's Spirit.

On Monday morning I sat in the back row of the dining hall feeling a bit guilty about missing morning worship. Then I saw him in the front row near the window. It was just the two of us. I was overwhelmed — imagine me, observing the Savior. As John Michael Talbot sang on tape, "Healer of My Soul," while I was eating breakfast, I realized that he was bringing healing to me.

Joy came to me in the car on the way to the Jewish Center in Louisville where I was taking him. We were listening to a tape of Gregorian chants which he loved so much. He said that there was a kind of sadness in the music because "there is a feeling of having to give something up for a higher place." He paused, bowed his head and whispered a few words of prayer as he listened to each enchanting sound.

As he crawled out of the van, he said, "I know this is the last time I shall ever see you." Tears brimmed in my eyes. He smiled and vanished as we drove away.

You came unexpectedly, bent over at the waist in worn, wrinkled clothing; and in you I saw him offering the rarest of gifts — Love!

I'll never forget you.

Note: Madelin is a bag lady from Maryland who mysteriously showed up at the Abbey of Gethsemane during the time of a women's retreat in Trappist, Kentucky.

For the Love of Mark

Audrey L. Burkhalter
Kokomo

Taking the traditional wedding vows on December 19, 1964, was to be the foundation our family would build its home on. " . . . For better for worse, for richer or poorer, in sickness and in health. . . ."

On our list of doing everything right to make a marriage work—or so we thought—was to have completed our education and have a house for a home. Soon our first child was to join us. We had waited five years. . . . It takes a long time to get everything in order. Mark Edward arrived after a difficult birth, only to have many struggles just to live. Ed and I prayed if only this little boy could live, I would stay home to take care of him, and Ed would further his education to be a school administrator. We realized that Mark's needs could be financially challenging. We knew we could do it if Mark could only live. Mark lived.

We learned early that we did not like labels unless they helped to provide a program for Mark to learn or receive care to make him stronger. In our family Mark was first a child; his problems were secondary. In other words, he was not a "problem child" to us. But life was not easy! Andrea, our second child, came home from school one day and kept silent until bedtime. Then she cried. She had been asked to share about her "retarded" brother. She did not know why the teacher had called him that. She looked at us and asked, "Is he retarded?" We, with pain in our hearts, said "Mark is Mark. We do not use labels for people, but we must realize that others do not always understand." This was the same little girl who, when asked in a kindergarten car pool, "What can your brother do?" answered quickly and with pride, "If you hold his hand, he gives love." After all, in the car he had only clapped his hands and squealed for others to see. The children did not know that perhaps a breeze or maybe, just maybe, an angel had spoken to him and filled his heart with gladness—but Andrea knew.

Three years after Andrea was born, with doctors' input and more prayers, we had Sheri Lynn. Both girls loved, played with, and were proud of their brother—whether at home, at church, or in public. This close bonding was soon to cause severe pain.

As Mark grew older and weaker, more needs were required: a feeding tube, a suction machine, blood transfusions and, later, oxygen. For two years, nurses provided excellent care and became a part of our family circle. But, money and insurance—or a lack thereof—made yet another decision for us. Mark had to go to a new home—a nursing home. Mark was nineteen, an age when most children leave home either for college or to be on their own, but this was not our son's case. How could God do this or allow it? We had totally accepted Mark, and now he must leave us.

Walter, our pastor who had welcomed this family to his church a few years previous, was there to greet us at Mark's new home. My heart was broken for a moment. I felt defeated, as if a committed battle to love, to accept, and to care for Mark had been lost. Mark had to leave our protective environment for this world of the unknown. Pastor Walter's prayer was to help us heal the hurt, just as he had when we came to his church several years before.

In a matter of days it felt as if our family was falling apart. Pastor Walt explained that our family was like a wheel, and a spoke had been taken out. Only our family can understand the intensity of such issues. Implications from well-meaning people that a stronger faith could heal Mark, almost destroyed us.

On the evening of November 26, we were asked to return to the hospital only to find Sister Camille reading scripture and having prayer with Mark. Sheri asked a nurse, "Is Mark going to die?" Her response was that the implications from his vital signs were that he would most likely not make it through the night. Sheri squeezed Mark's hand as she sang "You are My Sunshine." He left quietly. Our hearts were broken. Through our tears of sadness, we took time to also laugh and rejoice knowing that he could now run, play, breathe freely, and tell others in heaven, "Yeah, that's my family. They really loved me!" We, the four of us, thank God for Mark.

If you read this and also have a loved one requiring intense care, realize the need to surround yourself with people of faith, whether they're doctors, nurses, friends or church family. God will be there to support you. Your faith will see you through. Know the child is a gift on loan. Love and fulfill the needs the best you can. God will take him home all too soon. Until then, do your best, read and reread the Serenity Prayer. It says it all. God really loves each and every one.

Heroes, Guardians and God

Grace Conrad Liebert
New Albany

In the fall of 1993 my health began failing very fast. By mid January 1994, I was hemorrhaging badly. On a cold February 8, through sleet and snow, I was taken from the Floyd Memorial Hospital by ambulance to Indiana University Medical Center in Indianapolis. My husband, Melvin, and our son, Gary, followed behind the ambulance. Several vehicles had slid off the road, but we all made it safe and sound. The Lord was watching out for all of us!

I was seen by a team of transplant doctors and told the cause of my liver going bad was an inherited trait—too much iron in my blood which is called hemochrometosis. My liver and kidneys could not rid my body of toxins and I got ammonia in my brain. It messed up my thinking and I was not conscious at all times.

After undergoing all kinds of tests, my name was put on a list, and I received a "new" liver on March 3 that same year. The surgeon who put my liver in was one of my heroes and the other was the donor family. The donor was a twenty-eight-year-old man from Indiana.

During my hospitalization, I never saw the Lord, I never heard the Lord, but I knew he was with me. I put all my trust in him. I told him I would like to live, but if it was not his will, I was ready.

I was in intensive care March 3–22, and was not conscious during that time at all. The team of nurses in ICU were my "guardian angels," especially Toni, the nurse assigned to care for me. She told our sons she was the one that took care of patients the doctors thought may not live. When you are flat on your back, unconscious, tubes going everywhere, monitors being hooked up to you recording vitals, you are at the mercy of others. Your caregivers just have to be guardian angels. I did not remember Toni, but went back to visit her and the other nurses and received several hugs. They are always glad to see former patients and the progress they have made.

My condition now is—I feel great! I no longer have pain or feel bad. My strength and stamina could be better, but I have accepted my limitations and adjusted to them. Melvin and I are members of TRIO which is a support group not only for organ recipients, but donor families and those waiting to get transplants. We strongly urge everyone to become a donor.

A transplant is a very rough operation. It helps to have a positive outlook and a sense of humor. I felt all along the Lord was with me and I would recover. With his help, the doctors' knowledge, the nurses' care, the love and support of my family, and my attitude, I did survive.

The Lord has only asked me to do one thing and that is to give a blessing to the people as they leave the worship service such as, "Have a good week," "God bless you," etc. Of course they get hugs and handshakes along with it. I hope they can see the Lord through me.

Melvin and I had a very strong faith before my operation. I really believe the Lord used me to perform a miracle for the benefit of my family as well as the congregation at our church.

Holy Hands

Harold Leininger
Brownsburg

Last Sunday we sang: "These are holy hands, He's given us holy hands, He works through these hands, and so these hands are holy." As we sat in the sterile environment of an examining room, I observed the doctor carefully removing Andrea's bandages. The slightly graying 6' 3" physician then tenderly touched the wounds he had created through reconstruction surgery. With quiet reassuring words, he instilled hope as his fingers traced the area where he had work yet to do. Through the badly bruised and sutured tissue, he saw what we could not see because he understood what we did not understand. As a skilled plastic surgeon, he knows well the intricate components which come together to promote the process of healing. Truly, he exhibited the best in creatively uniting the art and science of medicine.

As I watched the doctor examine Andrea, I mysteriously was drawn to the form and shape of his hands. Something came over me. I caught sight of something I hadn't seen in fifty years. For the first time since my father's death in 1948, I caught a glimpse of my father's hands. The last time I saw and felt my father's hands was when I was a young boy. Shortly before my father died, he asked if I would help him to walk around his bed. With his six-foot three and one-half inch frame nearly bent double because of tuberculosis, he placed his long thirty-seven-year-old hands on my shoulders. In so doing I experienced the special touch of my father's love. It may sound uncanny to you, but Andrea's physician's hands transported me to my father's hands.

Our hands are holy hands. Just as the physician's hands helped my father to live again in my heart for a few moments, so do our hands enable others to touch the hands of God.

Kindred Spirits

Jacquie Reed
Fishers

A precious example of spiritual friendship in my life occurs each Monday when I gather with three other women. All four of us are in different occupations, we have different spiritual gifts, our personalities vary, and two churches are represented in membership. However, God works to bring people together, and each week we touch and encounter the place where God resides in each of us, at the level of the heart.

We begin our time with a few minutes of silence in which we become centered in God's presence. A candle is lit as a tangible symbol of God being with us. Then we explore the ways in which God has made his presence known throughout the week, we confess to temptations and weaknesses, we relate how the Holy Spirit is empowering our thoughts and actions, we challenge each other to discipleship in the kingdom, and we reveal ways in which God was encountered through reading scripture and/or books in study. Over the months, we have faced together illnesses of two members, serious surgery and lengthy hospitalization of one member's mother, challenges with college-age children, adjustment to new jobs, decisions regarding direction in life, and many others. We try to be Christ to each other—kindred spirits you might say. When one is down, the others gather intercessorily and frequently tangibly for uplifting; when there is joy, we celebrate!

Emilie Griffin in her book, *Clinging, The Experience of Prayer*, describes spiritual friendship with these words.

> Don't ask me where such a friend can be found. It is hardly a question of finding at all, for nothing we do can ever accomplish it. To find a spiritual friend is truly

to be chased down, smoked out of one's hiding place in the corner of existence and brought into the center, into the blazing presence of God.

This friendship is friendship with God, and with others because of God. It is a friendship not of the flesh, but of adoption, a spiritual bond that echoes Shakespeare's words in Hamlet. 'Those friends thou hast, and their adoption tried, Grapple them to thy soul with hoops of steel.'

Such a group illustrates clearly the words in Ecclesiastes 6:14,"A faithful friend is a sure shelter; whoever finds one has a rare treasure." Or in my words, this group is not only a circle of friendship, but a circle of God.

Mother's Hands

Nancy Gring
South Bend

In 1992, when I was on my Walk to Emmaus, our table group held hands as we prayed and sang. As I held the woman's hand next to me I was so thrilled to feel her hands, as they were just like I remembered my mother's dear hands to feel. I shall never forget this sensation and I remarked many times to my table partners about this pleasant soft hand experience. Not only did I renew my commitment to Christ during those three days but I also had other pleasant memories to take home with me.

At a later time we were having a special dinner to honor the women of our church, and I had promised to make up a large tray of apple slices for one of the desserts. I have made them in the past using a delicious recipe that many years ago my mother had written out on a three-by-five-inch card for me. The day I had to do the baking, I was frantic because I could not find my mother's apple slice recipe. I began a terrible journey through every cookbook that I owned looking for that recipe because it was truly a special one. In a cookbook that had been printed by another local United Methodist Church group, I found a recipe exactly like my mother's.

I was so happy that I called the person who had sold me the cookbook and thanked her for saving my skin that day. As my friend and I chatted about my solved dilemma of the lost-but-now-found recipe for my mother's special apple slices, she realized that she also remembered that recipe. My friend said to me, "You know, the woman who submitted that recipe was the woman who sat next to you during our Emmaus Walk. She was the lady who had the soft hands like your mother's."

My Angel Swims

James D. Hubbard
Gas City

As I dived into the depths of a water-filled abandoned stone quarry, I was unaware that my guardian angel was accompanying me. Suddenly, I ran into a solid wall, stopping my progress. When I tried to go to the surface, another solid wall was overhead. I was panicking when my special heavenly helper got me turned around and headed back the way I had come. Desperately, I clawed my way to the distant surface, aided by a hearty shove from my unseen but vigilant angel. With his help I was able to regain the surface. Still gasping for air, I lay on the bank, surrounded by my three teenaged companions. How close did death seem to all of us at that moment!

Later, we found out that, when the quarry was in operation, steel cars loaded with stone were hauled by a winch to the ground level. It was one of these cars—lying on its side—that almost became my tomb.

Quietly, soberly and in silence, we dressed and left the quarry. We have never returned.

Now, fifty years later, the Lord has blessed me with a wife, three children, eight grandchildren and seven great-grandchildren. All of us are still under the protection of a busier-than-ever agent from God.

Samaritan in a Truck

Patsy E. Fleener
Avon

A church meeting had been scheduled the evening I would need to drive to our daughter's, nearly three hours away. As chairperson of the meeting, I tried to keep the business moving along, and we finished at approximately 8:30 P.M. I left church, stopped at our home, picked up my suitcase, kissed my husband good-bye and left for Bloomington. I had traveled at night to our daughter's many times by myself and had no second thoughts about doing so.

Our granddaughter, Anne, was scheduled for surgery early the next morning, and I was to stay with our other grandchildren. I glanced at my watch and thought, no problem, I should make it by 12:00. Suddenly I saw a tan flash on the right front side of my car. I felt a thud and saw what appeared to be smoke coming from my steering wheel. My first thought was that the car was on fire and I needed to get to the side of the road and out of it. I looked out the rear mirror and could see nothing coming. I was able to drive to the side of the road, coming to rest under an overpass. Getting out of the car to inspect the damage, I saw I had no headlights and the front right side of my car was caved in. I had hit a deer. The air bag had come out so fast I had not realized that the "smoke" was chemicals from the bag and that the car was not on fire. I thought to myself, "Why didn't I let my husband buy me that cellular phone when he wanted? I certainly could use it now."

Several cars I tried to flag down passed by without stopping. I then realized how this must look. From the back of my car nothing appeared to be wrong. Here was a woman parked under a bridge alone on the interstate. I had certainly heard of scenarios like this before where would-be good Samaritans had been robbed or killed. I also realized that I was at the mercy of whomever might stop. I said, "God, I'm in your hands. Please help me. I can't do this by myself."

Finally as a semi truck passed me, I realized the driver was stopping. He pulled off the road, got out of his truck and began walking back toward me. I explained what had happened; whereupon, he replied he needed to get me off the interstate as there were tornado warnings out for the area. Inspecting my car, he felt if I could start it perhaps I could drive to the first exit which was approximately two miles away. He would radio the Farmer City police to meet us. He gave me a light to plug in the lighter so I could see the road to follow him.

To my surprise, the car started. I was able to drive to where I could safely pull off the road. A policeman was there to take me to the station to report the accident and to contact my family.

As I was thanking the trucker, I asked for his name and trucking company so that I might write and let them know how appreciative I was of his kindness and helpfulness. The trucker said, "You know it. I know it and the Lord knows it. That is all that is important." With that he climbed into his truck and left.

After I was picked up by my daughter and our granddaughter's surgery was over, I was checked at the hospital for the contusions on my arms from the air bag and bruises on my chest from the seat belt. The doctor at the hospital said it was a miracle that I lived to tell about it, since many don't after hitting deer.

The next day as my husband, who had traveled over to make arrangements for the car and to get me, and I were returning home he commented that angels appear in many forms. I couldn't have agreed with him more.

I strongly felt the power of Christ's arms around me when I put myself in his hands. The trucker was indeed an angel sent to rescue me.

Stepping Out on Faith

Minnietta Millard
Indianapolis

The phone call to him was to be about poetry, but that topic slid into the background when I discovered that "Ronald" was depressed—close to the point of suicide. I had always admired him for the way he lived so bravely and dynamically in a body that from birth had confined him to a wheelchair. Ronald had completed seminary and preached in a commanding, rumbling bass voice in spite of the fact that it would take him a full hour to pick up a dropped pen.

In response to his depression, I offered to loan him the money to attend a workshop that had been most helpful in my life. When I also offered to drive him the seven hours to get him there, he agreed.

At a loading dock, four men maneuvered Ronald in his electric wheelchair into my van. Ronald trusted me completely, but I could see a look in the other men's faces that said, "How in the world is she ever going to accomplish this?"

I had no doubts. As I had expected, at every step of the way when I needed four strong men to lift Ronald out of or into the van, God provided. Mid-morning at one such transfer, my look in all four directions disclosed only one person, a baggy-pants teenager crossing the street. I asked him for help; he agreed. As he paced uncomfortably to wait, I entered a bar whose only occupants were two men working behind the counter. I asked for assistance and they replied, "Lady, we're paid to work behind this counter." But they reluctantly agreed to help if we'd hurry and get it over with. As we reached the van, a man in full business attire dashed from a motel; I nabbed him.

As these four men took in Ronald's condition and his trust in this strange woman, their countenances changed. They lifted him from the van in silence and with great care; it was as if this unlikely group had become a bonded community for those few seconds.

At my final drop off, Ronald wasn't able to operate his wheelchair due to dents from the inexperienced lifters of the week. It had happened before and he knew how it could be fixed with a pliers. I pushed him into a motel lobby where I explained the situation to the receptionist and asked for pliers. She started to say, "Sure, let me page the repairman," but before she finished the last word, in through the door rushed the repairman — pliers in hand.

He fixed the wheelchair, stood to leave, looked into my eyes and in his face I saw the face of Christ. It was a holy moment as are all moments when we put our trust in God.

The Kayla Connection

Heather Olson-Bunnell
Roanoke

Eyes darting around the room, Kayla entered the narthex tightly clutching her registration card. She had responded to a flier advertising Kids Club, that Columbia City United Methodist Church sent home through her elementary school. She quickly joined in the fun and fellowship.

At the end of the first day's program, Kayla was left standing alone. No parent arrived to claim her. She came on the school bus with friends and followed them to the church. Those children walked home without her. Now tears began forming in her five-year-old eyes. I quickly walked over and put my arms around her shaking shoulders. Thus began a very special relationship in my life.

Taking her into my office, I scanned the registration forms and found an incomplete one with her name attached. With so many children that first day, no one had noticed the blank spaces on her form. No phone number was listed. When I questioned her, Kayla responded, "We don't have one." "No problem," I replied. "Just tell me where you live," as I noticed only the street name, not number, recorded. "I don't remember," and she began to cry. "No problem," I repeated. "Take my hand and we'll walk up and down the street until we find it."

As I began leading Kayla outdoors, the phone rang. It soon became apparent I was needed in the office for a while. Our choir director, Toni, offered to walk her home. Toni came back and shared that Kayla lived in a very small apartment above a furniture store downtown.

The next week, Kayla returned to Kids Club with her mother. She introduced Toni and me as her "two new friends." Her mother thanked us for taking such good care of Kayla and offered to bake cookies for the club.

Kayla was like a sponge absorbing water. She never got tired of hearing Bible stories. After Kids Club, she would come and ask me if those stories about Jesus were really true. On other days of the week, she would stop in my office to give me a hug or to show me her school papers. Sometimes I would see her playing in the street, when I walked downtown. She would be sitting on a curb playing with stones or a stick. I always stopped to chat with her.

Kayla started inviting other children to come to Kids Club. Since she didn't have a phone at home, she would ask permission to use mine. Our secretary called her "our youngest evangelist."

One day I was working at my desk when she was using the telephone. She turned to me and said: "Pastor Heather, tell him you serve dinner." I tried to explain to Kayla that I couldn't do that, as we served a snack: peanut butter sandwiches, fruit or cheese and crackers. She interrupted me and pleaded: "But John will come if you say he'll get dinner. He's hungry just like me."

When I shared that information with our Kids Club staff, we began to change our focus. Feeding hungry kids became a priority! We also intentionally began an outreach to families who had less than many of our members.

Sometimes when we discovered a need, we referred the families to a helping agency. We also began a hands-on ministry to those families. That ministry has included providing school clothes for children, emergency food, getting a telephone installed and granting scholarships to our new preschool. When you minister to a child, you minister to a family!

Last Christmas, Kayla brought me a present wrapped in newspaper. It was heavy. I wondered how she carried it upstairs to my office. "Isn't that the most wonderful present you've ever seen, Pastor Heather?" I assured her it certainly was, as I began to unwrap it. Inside was a gray brick. Kayla, my five-year-old street kid had probably found it in her alley.

I proudly display that gift on my desk to remind me of the Kaylas of the world who have never heard the stories of Jesus. The Good News is too good to keep to ourselves. Pass it on.

"Let the little children come to me; do not stop them; for it is to such as these that the kingdom of God belongs,"(Mark 10:14).

Two on a God Quest

Bel Skoc
Westville

It was the summer of 1989. We had just moved into the neighborhood. A few doors down another family had moved in just before us.

I don't remember what brought Charmaine and I together, but to say the least our relationship was rocky at best. We moved to get away from people; and she, feeling alone, needed people. That combination escalated into a terrible argument one day. "Quit bothering me!" and "How could you say that to me?" echoed in our empty hearts.

Now to back up a little, she and I were not foreign to God. We knew him as the judging and condemning God. The God of impossible rules and "thou shalt nots." I had read a book that talked about a loving God, and I had given it to Charmaine. That day there was a stirring in us that would not let this be the end. Within hours we came to repentance and forgiveness. First to each other and then to God. We discovered a loving God. That triggered in us an unquenchable thirst and drive to find out all we could about this God. We pursued anything that talked about a God of love. We started down a path of Eastern philosophy, a "higher power" that was very inviting but left us empty. We kept trying to rise above the world by having a higher conscience and be like God.

But something was missing. We read about how Jesus was just this nice guy—a really high-up guy but not the son of God. In each religion there was always someone between Jesus and God.

Another friend, Cathy, knew Jesus and told her pastor about what we were doing. He immediately set up a meeting with us, and over a period of time set us on the right path—a path we were taught as children—Jesus is God's son.

The hunger and thirst for the truth accelerated—all we wanted was the truth. Charmaine and I gave up everything to find the truth. Houses got dirty, laundry piled up and meals were thrown together. Everything we had taken pride in now was squeezed in between the quest for God.

Then the unthinkable happened. Our husbands were also left out. Drastic measures were taken as our husbands thought they had lost us to God.

That started a whole new life for us. As we struggled to put our families back together, we grew deeper and deeper in our knowledge and relationship with God, Jesus and the Holy Spirit. We witnessed healing and humility. We saw firsthand God working in our families. My mother who lives with us came to Christ at age eighty-six. Charmaine saw her husband turn his life around and be delivered from alcohol.

Charmaine and I repented together. Grew together. Learned to trust together. We are so thankful that God brought us together, and every day is a day we grow in the Lord.

Part Four

THE MANY SHADES OF GRACE

A Miracle to Deliver

M. Dawn Buss
Highland

"It's approximately 2:30 A.M. Friday morning, January 29, 1993. I'm wide awake, not able to sleep. I've reminisced about the happenings of the day before.

"I feel as though God has given me a basket full of emotions; and emotions keep jumping out at me. Exuberance, anger, elation, frustration, deprivation, depression, excitement, joy, pain, sorrow, love and confusion to name just a few. Thoughts keep flowing freely through my head. Visions I can't keep from—hopes and dreams I never thought would come true, unanswered prayers finally being answered.

"Thursday, January 28, 1993, I met my birth mother! It has certainly been a mixed bag of emotion for me and I hadn't anticipated it being this difficult or painful. I've been given a new tricycle but told not to ride it. I want to get on and just go to town. Perhaps, I'm moving too fast, expecting too much of others and myself. But it's Christmas and I'm not done opening my presents. I want more! I want to see more and I want to know more. Even more important, I want to give more . . . more of what I have to give.

"I want to take forty-some years, wrap it up with all its joys, sorrows and experiences and give it back to that part of my family that I never knew. Not to dump it, but to share it; it's all a part of me. It is me. Me. Yes, me! Then I want—and I guess I really need—for all of them to wrap up their joys, sorrows, and experiences for forty some years and share them with me.

"These rushes of emotion are a real roller coaster ride. . . . The fear of rejection and losing all of them again is almost more than I can bear. I don't want to push myself on any of them nor force myself into their lives. My hope is that they would want me in their lives as well. Perhaps my expectations are too high. I'd love to be a part of their lives, if they'll have me.

"I'm down on my knees to God and pray they do, thanking God for such a miracle. Forgive me, God, if I am moving too fast. I believe I am out of control. I feel like I have plenty of logic and I can look and examine all angles and variables. I just can't control the pangs in my heart. What have you done to me? Certainly, you have answered my prayer showing your great love for me. Yesterday, you turned my world completely upside down. What will today bring?"

I wrote that over four years ago and since that time have come to grips with the emotion and the letdown of hopes and dreams that were never meant to be. God knew that. And yet, I kept asking—persistent about finding a mother who, perhaps, was regretful for what she had done.

Instead I found a shallow, empty shell of a woman who, because of the loss of another child thirty-five years before, could not open her arms and heart to me. She was so overcome with grief and guilt for her part in the death of that child that perhaps I was not the answer to her own prayers. I forgave her for not choosing to keep me—at birth and now. I let go of the anger, frustration, depression, pain, sorrow and confusion.

I have since learned God did not give me a miracle to make me whole and happy, but to show his love through me by forgiving those who hurt me. God gave me a miracle that day all right, it just wasn't the one I expected it to be. He gave me a charge to keep, and I believe I did as he wanted me to do. Perhaps now she will know of God's divine love for us and begin to realize that God has forgiven her, too. That is my prayer now. And this prayer is so much more satisfying in realizing I was given a miracle, not to keep, but to deliver.

After the Killing

Lynne DeMichele
Indianapolis

Knowing its terrible story, I had gone on a Saturday to St. Peter's Lutheran Church in Monrovia, Liberia. I had come to this troubled West African country as its long civil war was winding down, to report on the status of the mission schools there. The church compound was eerily serene, lifeless really, sealed behind its wall. News reports had said 800 refugees, perhaps even more, had been hacked and shot to death in that place only a year ago. In a blood rage over the murder of their leader Samuel Doe, his soldiers had taken revenge on the city.

One infamous summer night at the height of the frenzy, they stormed into the sanctuary, barred the doors and began the slaughter. Babies were thrown into a well behind the parsonage. No one was spared.

Their bodies lay where they had fallen until late autumn, when at last a truce between rebel factions and the deposed government's troops was established. By the time the victims could be buried in mass graves in the church yard, identification was impossible. The names of some who died there will never be known. Yet every living soul in the city had loved someone who perished there.

The church compound had remained sealed since the burial, but the walls of the church and its buildings bore testimony with their dark stains and sprays of bullet holes. Moving among the debris of that night's violence, I walked carefully to avoid stepping on a few small bones that remained. A grisly stench still hung in the air a year after the killing. As I stood in that place, the full horror of what had happened swept over me like a fire. The impressions burned and there was no respite from them or from the realization of the monstrous evil they evoked.

Next morning, reluctantly I approached the United Methodist church nearby where I'd planned to worship with its Bassa tribe congregation—"reluctant" in the way one hesitates to face those who grieve or suffer greatly. Many of those buried in St. Peter's yard were Bassa. And I knew that each one I'd be praying with that morning had lost many close relatives and friends in the previous year's violence.

I didn't know how to worship with people who had suffered so immeasurably. There seemed an enormous distance between the God of my safe, sedate home church in Indianapolis and whomever was watching over this ravaged city a hemisphere away. I sat in a back pew with my reporter's note pad, feeling apart from what was about to happen.

Then the singing began. I couldn't understand the words, but the message was unmistakable. These people had thrown back their heads and lifted up their hands to make the most joyful noise I'd ever heard. Amazingly, they were celebrating. They were expressing, flat-out, the joy of their deliverance, their trust in God and the enduring love that bound them.

I don't remember putting away my note pad during the service; I only remember being drawn to my feet by the spirit that filled that place. We were clapping and singing together—moving with the sounds of the accompanying drums and bells. Then, after the sermon, we shared the Holy Feast together. I felt a part of the whole.

Somehow at that moment, I understood the mystery of God's grace in a new and infinitely beautiful way. The Liberian Christians, my brothers and sisters, had given me a gift of supreme value that day.

It has changed me.

An Answer on the Sand

Jill Bunning
Indianapolis

Like many, I had a very rocky adolescence. I usually turned to God only to beg for selfish things, most often involving the feelings of a boy I "loved." My faith took a turn, however, in the face of a frightening depression.

My senior year in high school, I started dating Elliott (not his real name), a guy I had been friends with for two years. Our relationship got serious very fast, and we spent the summer following my graduation together nearly every day.

When I went to college that fall, however, things got bad. Elliott wasn't in college and didn't understand why I needed to go. The school was nearly a four-hour drive from our home, and I didn't have a car. He found it more and more difficult to justify having to drive down and see me all the time and became jealous of my college life and friends.

Eventually, Elliott became mentally and emotionally abusive to me. Often, he would call me and question everything I did that day. I had to give him my class schedule, and if I wasn't in my room when he thought I should be, he would call later, infuriated. He even had me paged in the cafeteria once, demanding to know why I wasn't in my room waiting for his call. When he came to see me, he would criticize my clothing. I couldn't wear anything but loose-fitting shirts, buttoned to my neck, nor was I "allowed" to wear make-up, lest other guys look at me. I couldn't even go barefoot because I would be showing skin!

I became severely depressed, controlled by this obsessive behavior. I stopped socializing or doing anything that would take me out of my room when Elliott might call. I spent most of my time looking out my window and crying. I began to pray that God would help me understand, would help me to be a better person.

One Thursday night I got a call from Elliott. He demanded that I come to see him. I balked, having no car and needing to study that weekend. Then he threatened to kill himself if he couldn't see me—the ultimate power play. What could I do? I felt I had to go. After my last class Friday, I walked to the bus depot and bought a ticket. But when I reached my hometown, exhausted and weak, Elliott could only berate me.

We drove to Lake Michigan to talk. It was a dark night with just a sliver of the moon above. While Elliott continued to verbally attack me, I sat motionless and stared at the moon. I prayed for an answer to my emptiness. I truly felt that no one really loved me, that no one would listen. Then an answer came, dark and ugly, from the depths of my depression. I stood and slowly began walking through the sand toward the Great Lake. I was not planning to stop until I was swallowed by the water.

When I reached the place where the lake dampened the sand, I found myself suddenly on my knees. I honestly felt as if I had been driven to my knees by a great force. I knew it was God. He had touched me, made me stop. When I looked up at the moon again, I felt a great hope and a great relief to still be alive. Most of all, I knew that no matter what, God loved me. I found the strength to end my relationship with Elliott and move on with life, on the shoulders of a new faith.

Flowers under Snow

Shirley Hanna
Pittsboro

My sister, Judy, died on Mother's Day of a drug overdose. We buried her on Thursday, as her daughter, her mother, her three grandchildren and her family wept.

The sister I knew died a long time ago. She started doing drugs when she was eighteen and died when she was forty-six.

She never saw God's wonderful creations no matter how many people tried to help her. She never saw the greenness of spring, the happy chirping of birds or the sun's warm shine. I used to say that Judy was one of God's lost sheep. The minister giving her service referred to that also.

The last time I saw Judy she looked really bad. I was expecting to see her looking bad at the funeral, but instead she looked very much at peace.

What bothered me was that I could not remember any good times with my sister and neither could my brother. God has helped me slowly remember those good times. They were buried underneath all the bad times and hurt she and the drugs had created. They are slowly coming up like flowers underneath a cold snow.

I wish Judy's dependence and depression had not hidden God's creation from her. I wish she had been able to see the sun shine.

I said one hundred times I would not shed a tear for Judy because of the hurt the drugs made her do. But those tears were shed, whether I wanted them to or not. My eyes will be more open to God, now—for myself and for my dead sister.

Following the White Fields

Audra Piner
Muncie

My life has been an incredible journey of faith. I was born a VPPK (Very Poor Preacher's Kid), third in a family of nine children. I grew up in a Christian atmosphere; all my relatives and friends were Christians and attended church and Sunday School. We were not forced to go, we just went, as the only activities in those days were the church and PTA. I was baptized at the age of sixteen by my father in a little creek, while church friends and family stood on the banks singing "Shall We Gather at the River?" However, one cannot inherit salvation.

Early in my marriage we moved to the little town of Parker City, east of Muncie. We were unchurched at that time. One day someone came to the door and invited us to Sunday School at the nearby Methodist Church. We went and there my journey of faith began. One day someone invited me to the Esther Circle. I went although I had no idea what it was. But I did know that I needed friendship, fellowship and companionship. By this time, my husband, Gene, was overseas in the Second World War and I would not see him for three years. With two little boys, my life was lonely and frightening from time to time.

In the fall of 1944, I attended a district meeting of the Women's Society of Christian Service (that was what it was called at that time). I can remember, almost exactly, the pew in which I was sitting. The speaker was a returned missionary from Mozambique, with beautiful snow-white hair and a radiance of countenance I shall never forget. She spoke of the "fields being white with harvest and the laborers few" and then she quoted from the book of Romans, 10:13–16.

> ". . . for whosoever shall call upon the name of the Lord shall be saved. How then shall they call on him in whom they have not believed? And how shall they believe in him of whom they have not heard? And how shall they hear without a preacher? And how shall they preach, except they be sent? As it is written, 'How beautiful are the feet of them that preach the Gospel of peace and bring glad tiding of good things.'"

God spoke to me in those verses. At first I argued silently as to why I could not go—no car, no college education, two little boys, no husband and little money. But God said to look at it again. I did not have to go, but I could tell, send, give, and pray; and it was at that moment I promised to go where he wanted me to go, say what he wanted me to say and do what he wanted me to do. From that day on doors and windows have been opened that I never dreamed possible for a VPPK. I became involved in local, district, conference, state and regional organizations and movements and participated in numerous mission study tours to Southeast Asia, South Africa and the Holy Land.

More is yet to come in this, my fourscore year. I have been selected to teach "Brazil" in the summer School of Christian Mission. More privileges and honors have come my way than space allows. All because someone touched me with the gospel of Christ.

Heart Sparks

Robert L. Wells
New Albany

March 4, 1995, is a date that changed my life. Our daughter was home from college to celebrate her birthday, and—little did she know—a dinner was planned to announce her engagement. This is where my life changed beyond anything imaginable.

My only conscious memory is driving out of Centenary United Methodist Church parking lot after a Lay Speakers Training event. I do not remember the drive home or entering the house. Our seventeen-year-old son, Chad, was soon to perform a task that will forever bond us in ways beyond belief. He wanted to drive me to our new barber shop. Within two blocks from our home, I began to shake and collapsed against the dashboard. Chad stopped our automobile, felt for my pulse and rushed me directly to Floyd Memorial Hospital Emergency Entrance, blowing the horn for help.

As a nurse opened the car door, I rolled out on the ground. I had suffered "aborted sudden cardiac death" due to a severe drop in my potassium. Inside the emergency room, the medical staff shocked my heart four times before they were able to jump start it. Once stabilized, I was admitted to the Cardiac Care Unit unaware of any of these events.

As I began to regain consciousness Sunday morning, I noticed the bright morning sun outside my hospital window. Unable to speak, I wrote questions on a clipboard the nurse gave me. "Where am I? What happened to me? Where are my wife and children?"

My family and medical team quickly assembled around my bed checking monitors, intravenous levels and the ventilator. I could only blink my eyes or squeeze their hands to respond. After a heart catheter-ization, I was transferred to Jewish Hospital in Louisville, Kentucky. On March 13, I underwent surgery and received a transvenous auto-matic implantable cardiac defibrillator. Thank God for modern medicine and Christian doctors and nurses.

Since then I have resumed my normal work load as well as both local and district church functions as district lay leader with few restrictions and am involved in Heart Sparks, a support group for defibrillator patients.

Life the second time around is beyond belief. I am so blessed. You see our son, Chad, was born prematurely and doctors predicted his mental ability would be one degree above a vegetable. A life of prayers has allowed Chad a normal life and the insight to save my life.

I am not sure why I survived. Doctors have told me only about 20 percent of cardiac sudden death patients survive without permanent brain damage. Since then I have had the privilege to walk my daughter Holly down the aisle, a radiant bride, and entrust her to our wonderful son-in-law. I was able to sing at their wedding, and I shed tears of joy as she graduated this May from Eastern Kentucky University. Also Chad, my hero, graduated from New Albany High School and started college.

Without endless love, support, patience and care from my beautiful wife Carolyn, life would be without value. My minister, church and choir family, friends, and work associates are the safety net of God's love and redeeming grace. This has launched my faith to higher levels. God has given me a rare new purpose to have each moment to live wisely and to its fullest.

Pickup Full of Blessings

Minnietta Millard
Indianapolis

Her son had been killed while serving his country. Faith ran deeper than pain for this Lakota woman. After one year of mourning and preparation, she was ready for a "give away" in honor of the deceased. In my Caucasian culture it was expected that the bereaved family would be the recipient of gifts, money, flowers and food from friends and community. In contrast, this low-income mother, with the help of family and friends, had spent the whole year sewing quilts, making beaded jewelry and saving money to purchase food and gifts. All of this filled a pickup truck to overflowing for this special celebration beneath the sun on the prairie earth.

The number of guests swelled as the day progressed. The hungry were fed with stew and fried bread; no one was turned away, whether invited or not. The day was filled with eating, traditional dancing and fellowship. By the time farewells were sounded, each of the hundreds of persons had been given a gift by the grieving mother.

My ability to be a gracious receiver was sorely tested, as the beauty of this totally unselfish giving clashed with my calculated tithe and selected charities. Voices of cheers and remorse battled within me as I observed this mother with an empty pickup truck and a filled spirit. I saw a proud Lakota woman once again living out the truth of her faith, that the shattering pain of personal grief could be turned into uniting joy through the lifestyle of unreserved giving.

That day I returned home with many gifts—not just the beautifully crafted offerings, but the gifts of being blessed and being forever changed.

Sanctuary

Patricia Ashman
Muncie

I sit in your beautiful sanctuary, Lord.
It's Saturday morning . . . no one is here except me.
The silence gives me time to think and pray;
Time to know that you are Lord, you are God!
This is holy ground.
It was built to glorify you.
Your Spirit dwells and reigns in this place.
I feel your presence, Lord.
I know that anywhere you are is holy ground,
But this is somehow special to me.
It is truly the sanctuary of my heart and of my soul.
I have come here in pain and left with joy.
I have come here with questions and left with answers.
I have come here hurt and angry and found release and peace.
I have come here with emptiness and left fulfilled.
I have come here with a hard heart and left softened by your holy
    touch.
I have come here with joy just to praise your name.
I have come here a sinner and left forgiven.
I have come here selfishly and left, leaving self behind.
I have come here with burdens and left with those burdens lifted.
I have received messages of love and hope from the pulpit;
Often they seem like they are only for me . . . yet I know others
    experience this too.
I have been challenged from the same pulpit and left with
    determination to change, to grow.
I have experienced beautiful soul-stirring music and sung simple
    scripture songs that come directly from your Word.

It is here at the piano where my fingers have gained strength that
Parkinson's disease would rob me of.
It is here that I worship with the body of Christ called Center Chapel.
It is here where I reach out my hand to find it taken by a brother or
sister in Christ.
It is here where your Spirit has touched me in special ways.
I sit in your beautiful sanctuary, Lord. Thank you for meeting me here.

Sin of Omission

Marion Tewksbury
Indianapolis

As I sat there in the pew, the feeling of despair and heartache
consumed me. I had been tortured with guilt for months now. Why
hadn't I told Mandy about Jesus and his love for her? Now it was too
late. I would never be able to make amends.

The picture of those happy teenagers laughing and dashing across
the sands at the resort in Florida was ever vivid in my mind. I knew
Mandy was troubled and having problems at home. Yet, the stories that
she told my daughter, Cindi, seemed so extreme I asked myself, "Could
any mother be that cruel?" I debated talking to Mandy and to her
mother, but dismissed the thought as putting my foot in where it did not
belong. Still something kept prodding me to tell Mandy about Jesus —
after all, a Jewish child probably knew nothing of him.

Christmas vacation was warm in Florida. We all enjoyed the holiday
and returned home, I to my teaching job, and the girls to school. Then
came that fateful day. The telephone rang early. Did I know that the
police and ambulance had been at Mandy's early that morning?

I left for school without knowing any more, but at noon I called a
friend. The news was devastating. Mandy had taken her life by swal-
lowing a handful of her mother's sleeping pills. The neighborhood was
shattered, as was the school. Cindi was one of her closest friends. Did she
even suspect how troubled Mandy was? No, she just knew the horrible

things that Mandy said her mother made her do, like lapping up the milk off the floor when she had accidentally spilled it. And now this lovely young girl was gone. Why hadn't I shared the love of Jesus with her?

These thoughts had tormented me for weeks — why, why hadn't I told her? I kept asking myself this question over and over. Now as I was moving toward the kneeling rail, I kept thinking of that dear child. Would this feeling of gloom and remorse consume me forever?

I knelt in preparation for Communion, and as I did I said, "Oh Lord, please, please forgive me. I was so wrong not to share you with Mandy. I am so sorry."

As I uttered those words it was as though a mantle of warmth and peace floated down over me from above. I felt a calmness and warmth inside, and as I got up to leave, I knew I had been forgiven.

I have thought of Mandy many times since, but never in that agonizing way, because I know that she is with God. I also know I have been given the gift of his infinite grace and forgiveness.

Standing on the Promises

Kathryn Leth
Staunton

God can use anyone who allows herself to be used. I am currently a part-time local pastor, appointed to a small rural church.

Eight years ago I wanted to die. I had just been diagnosed with lupus. My knees were so bad that I had to use a wheelchair; I had to give up my career as a nurse; and my children were grown and no longer needed me.

But God had other plans. Through a variety of people and circumstances I found a reason to live, had knee surgery and looked to the Lord for career guidance.

Driving home from Indianapolis one day the Lord called me into the ministry. I argued for weeks because I didn't think I would be physically able to do the things that a pastor must do. But God assured me that he does not call the equipped, but equips the called.

I finally answered the call, and as I do what the Lord wants me to do, he enables me physically to get through it. It's difficult for me to stand for more than a few minutes without pain in my artificial knees and arthritic hips, but on Sunday mornings when I am behind the pulpit, I feel no pain. I used to be very shy, but as I get up in front of my congregation, all fear leaves and peace is present.

No, God has not healed me completely or instantly but he has healed me. He heals me spiritually day by day and physically as necessary.

If God can use me, he can use you!

Sunflower Colors

Barbara K. Cross
Fort Wayne

Have you ever looked closely at a sunflower—a big, beautiful, yellow sunflower? I looked closely at one when my youngest son, Nathan, asked me to help him pick one out in our garden. He wanted to enter it in his school's flower show, so I looked for a long time trying to pick out the largest and the most beautiful sunflower. In fact, he won the blue ribbon for the largest sunflower entered which brought him great joy. However, I never imagined that someday I would look like a big, beautiful, yellow sunflower.

It was on a Thursday morning, when I looked in the bathroom mirror at myself and saw the color of my skin and eyes which were yellow, just like a sunflower. Being a teacher in the Nursery School and Parents' Day Out program at my church in Fort Wayne, I thought to myself, "How the children would love to see me now." I would fit perfectly for our "color days" in October. But God had something else in mind for me. After several doctor appointments, blood tests, X-rays, a visit to the emergency room, and finally a trip to Indiana University Medical Center in Indianapolis, I was diagnosed with auto-immune hepatitis. It is a rare disease with an unknown cause, where my immune system is attacking my liver. It was necessary for me to spend three months at home until my blood count returned to normal, away from the people I loved, away from the children I loved, away from the church I loved—but closer to the God I loved.

Not only was my immune system attacking my liver at that time, I was fighting against God's call in my life. I had felt God's call to go into the ministry, but being an older, married woman with three sons I did not pursue it, because of my own personal weaknesses and fears. How could God expect me to leave what I loved doing to follow His call at my age? How could God use me, a sinner? I had used every excuse in the book not to listen to God. In fact, I told the new pastor at our church when I talked to him after my illness about going into the ministry, "This is not me!" How right I was. It was not me, it was God working through me. It took this disease and the three months I spent at home to bring me to my knees and to surrender my life totally to God.

When they saw me at Indiana University Medical Center in Indianapolis, my condition was so critical that plans were being made for a liver transplant if the medication did not work. I remember the nurse saying to me, "Don't be afraid." She was a nurse in the liver transplant unit who asked to take my picture for her records of before and after patients. Then I remember answering her, "I'm not afraid, God will take care of me." Those words came out of my mouth, but I know they were God's words.

I also remember the pastor calling and asking me if I would sing at the Christmas Eve Service. The medication I was taking for the disease was a steroid and had affected my voice. Instead of being a soprano, I was now a bass. However, I told him I would try. Singing "O Holy Night" is a favorite song of mine, but it took the power of the Holy Spirit to witness through me that night that Jesus Christ truly was born, that Jesus Christ lives in our heart if we believe in him, and that Jesus Christ can use anyone to sing his praises if we put all our trust in him.

I am now enrolled in seminary taking my first course after twenty-seven years of not being in a college classroom. Again, another miracle of God. Just ask Virginia, the woman I talked with the day I visited. Before I left she left she said to me, "Someone is watching over you." I replied, "I know, God is watching over me," and then I asked her if I could give her a hug.

In those three months, God made me a sunflower for him that was humbly called to color the world with his Good News of unconditional love, amazing grace, and faithfulness. May I glorify and honor him in everything I do.

The Color of Brotherhood

Jacob C. Williams
Forest Park, Ohio

There we stood, facing each other. It had been more than three decades since I had vowed to kill him on sight. He was my childhood tormentor.

I, a Black boy of ten years of age and he, a Caucasian young man of twenty-two or more years of age. I could never forget his racial gibes and taunts and humiliating sneers. He had performed his executions before laughing crowds, while I carried water for the local baseball games at the Mill Field in my hometown in Martin's Ferry, Ohio.

My family consisted of five brothers, one sister and our widowed mother who had fled to this Ohio River industrial city to escape the experience of losing our father who was slain by unknown Whites in a little turpentine camp town in the state of Alabama. A year or so later, her father—our grandfather—was shot down in the rural grocery store while purchasing ten cents-worth of black-eyed peas.

Hurt, lonely and povertied beyond description, I cringed with a strange, agonizing, helpless fury. I went home which was located on the edge of the Mill Field baseball diamond. I met our mamma who was standing at the backdoor wondering why I was returning home before the game had ended. I'd had a job of carrying water for the baseball players for forty cents a game. I cried out to her with a terrible rage. "Mamma, I swear to God, as soon as I get a chance, I swear that I'm going to kill that dirty rotten honky for hurting me so bad every time that I carry water."

Now middle-aged and living far away, my childhood antagonist learned of the tragic death of my nephew who had drowned in the waters of the Ohio River where, earlier, we had also lost our only sister.

She and my older brother had been trying to cross the river to the West Virginia side to pick blackberries.

I was overwhelmingly disturbed during the day of my nephew's funeral. My antagonist and I stared at one another in the middle of the church where the body of the thirteen-year-old boy lay in state. My oppressor was here once more! My twin brother's son, Esau, now counted among the members of my family who tragically met death in our pain-filled lives.

Without fear, the son of Hungarian immigrants and I, the offspring of my father met in the middle of the church where the body of my nephew lay. The divine power of God took the play. Both of us had experienced the power of God's emancipating love during the years of absence from one another. Tears sprung to the eyes of both of us as we remembered our youthful past. We grasped one another's hands. Words were not needed. We fell upon one another's shoulders and sobbed without shame. The White man sought and found forgiveness. The Black man sought and found reconciliation. I was now the pastor of the Saulters United Methodist Church in Terre Haute, Indiana, and my new friend was a member of a church in Cleveland, Ohio.

The Electric Train

Harold Leininger
Brownsburg

There is a Christmas which will remain forever engraved upon my soul. When I was eleven my father was in the Irene Bryon Sanatorium in Fort Wayne slowly dying of tuberculosis. The wonder drugs which we all take for granted today were just in the experimental stages. My father was fifty miles away from our home in Akron. Also we were not permitted to be with him because of the contagiousness of the illness. Therefore, it looked like a bleak Christmas for the Leiningers.

My Dad knew that I had admired my friend Don's Lionel train for a long time. Don was the local funeral director's son and his father had one of the best businesses in our village. Don's electric train had all the latest cars and equipment, the engine even puffed smoke. Knowing my deep desire to have a train, my father asked my mother and an older cousin to go downtown in Fort Wayne and purchase a train for me. Because of our family's financial condition at the time, it had to be a modest train with only a few cars and short track. Just to buy it was a sacrifice on my parent's part.

After purchasing the train, the night before Christmas mother and my cousin Gene visited Dad in the hospital. They took the train out of the box, set it up, and ran it around my father's bed. He was delighted.

The next morning as we celebrated Christmas at my grandparents, I was spellbound. There was the best gift ever under the tree—an electric train. It wasn't as elaborate as my friend Don's, but that didn't even cross my mind at that moment. I focused on one thought only, "Even though my Dad couldn't physically be with me for Christmas, he sent what he knew I would love. And what's more, he enjoyed it himself." That was the most precious gift I ever received as a child.

This holiday season I went up into my mother's attic at Akron. I found intact the train which my father had given me fifty years ago. Why is that gift so important to me even yet today? In the spring of 1948 my father died, yet his memory endures. Today as then he may be gone from me in body, but his loving presence remains. When I looked at that electric train, once again he lived within my heart.

When I think of my heavenly Father, I can not discern his physical presence. Yet, I'm always aware of his presence through the many gifts of love which are showered upon us daily. When I look at electric trains, I am always reminded of God's greatest gift at Christmas time.

Part Five

IN THE CRUCIBLE

Blessed Assurance

Neoma Colpitts
North Webster

Much of my life has been a journey in faith. In retrospect, I realize being raised in a Christian home and living with the faith of a very devoted spouse, as well as many Christian relatives and friends has influenced my journey. There are so many incidences in my life when, through faith and trust, I was blessed.

Without a doubt, my faith was the most severely tested when I learned my spouse was seriously and terminally ill. I wondered how I could get through what this would mean for both of us. Since he was a man of a very deep faith, I remember he said, "Neoma, one never knows what one can do, until he has to do it, trusting in God." And so, putting my faith in God, I knew I could do whatever I needed to do with his help, one day at a time. I did get through those difficult days until my husband's death, with an assurance that could only have come from God.

My next test of faith has had to do with the coping of all that the loss of a spouse entails. Each day, I put my life in God's hands, in faith that I will have the courage and strength to do what needs to be done.

God works in such wonderful and mysterious ways through family and friends, at the most unexpected times, to undergird the loneliness along the journey. Perhaps it will be an unexpected phone call, an invitation to dinner, a meaningful letter, some beautiful flowers, the hug of a granddaughter, a visit from a pastor or friends. Because of the unexpectedness of these, I know God hears my prayers and sends me many very special blessings as I daily pray for a deepened faith that will help me develop better coping skills and overcome any fears I have concerning this time in my life. I can remember saying, "As people of God, we are called to live by faith, instead of fear."

So, as I sit in my little house by the lake, where I can see so much of God in nature and spend time in meditation, I know God is with me and will never forsake me. This fact helps me continue to grow in my faith, and in the assurance God walks with me each day. I pray I will always remember to be grateful to God for His many blessings to me on my faith journey.

Bullies

Janet Jackson
Greensburg

While doing our Disciple Bible Study, I was reading in Genesis. When I came across the story of Isaac in chapter 26:17–22, it seemed like such a simple and not very significant story. But I remembered a time when God took that simple story and taught me how to be a better mother to my son, Brian.

Brian was in third grade. He had a meek personality which was the perfect type for bullies to gravitate to. He was having a problem with a certain boy picking on him on the school bus.

He would complain about this daily. Of course, I thought my duty was to fix this problem. I would tell him to be firm and tell that boy to stop, to sit somewhere else, or to tell the bus driver. None of these seemed to work so I decided to call this bully's mom.

"Oh please don't," my son pleaded, "that would only make things worse." In desperation one day I bellowed, "For crying out loud, Brian, this has gone on long enough. Just hit him back." He looked surprised and I was shocked at my own outburst, since it went against everything I taught him.

At the same time, I was studying Genesis and came across this story. Isaac was setting up his own territory and dug a well. These "bullies" came along and took over the well. Isaac would move along and dig another well. Again, bullies would come along and take over. This happened three times until he finally found a place, dug a well, and no one came along to take over.

After reading this, the Lord revealed to me that this was the right way for Isaac to deal with these bullies. He wasn't the warrior type. Neither is my son. I realized that Brian didn't want me to solve this problem, but to just listen.

I asked Brian if he hit this bully back, after another episode. He said, "No." I asked him if he wanted to hit him back. He looked at me with serious, innocent eyes and said, "No." I said, "All right," and that was it. Brian continued to ride the bus, the bully continued to punch, yet somehow things worked out, because Brian is sixteen years old today and he doesn't ride that bus anymore. Who knows when it finally stopped?

Brian still has a non-assertive personality, yet God can use him too, just as he used Isaac.

I think God has reminded me of this recently; because, now my thirteen-year-old daughter is having problems with friends, I am tempted to "fix" things. Yet, I know she will deal with things according to her personality, and I will listen and love her through it.

Coping Alone?

Beverly Lang
Indianapolis

My father passed away due to cancer. I had to suddenly assume responsibilities which my father had carried out. I was not sure that I could meet the demands that were placed upon me.

My situation was unique in that I was not married and did not have the support of a spouse or children. I have no brothers or sisters. My mother was too ill to help me with business decisions or funeral arrangements. I lived outside the Indianapolis area, and I had to take a leave from my teaching position. I was alone, but not alone. This may sound like a paradox, but I did have the Lord on my side.

Many friends, neighbors, relatives, colleagues at work, and business people helped me greatly. I discovered that I could handle many tough decisions, and efficiently take care of family business. As my attorney pointed out, "I was all over town making deals." This was certainly a new experience for me. I was greatly relieved to hear that my mother and our relatives approved of many of my decisions.

A few weeks after the funeral, a friend remarked that she could not believe how well I had coped with my father's death. She did not think that she could do as well.

I replied that my faith had really helped me. I did not think of my funeral plans as a Christian witness, but they were. I was just doing what I had to do for my dad. In times of crisis, Christians can be a "light of the world" for those who need encouragement and examples.

Corn Supper

Linda Hoopes
Osgood

As part of the process to be licensed as a local pastor, one has to take a two-week intensive course dealing with everything from "how to preach" to "how to serve The Lord's Supper." I was insecure about the course and concerned about being out of the pulpit two weeks straight just after becoming the pastor of two small Madison churches.

I had been out of school for almost twenty years. It turned out to be the two most exciting weeks of my life. I returned to the two small churches with new insights and a license in my hand. I was elated because the license allowed me to now serve Communion. This was an aspiration of mine ever since entering the ministry. My dream was to serve my first Communion to those church members who were too ill to attend church. And that is just what I did.

Ralph, seventy-nine, was a long-time member of one of the Madison churches. He was hard of hearing and emaciated. Ralph had stopped eating solid foods in February. There was no medical reason for Ralph's loss of appetite. The medical staff was baffled.

I will never forget that day. Ralph's wife, Marge, opened the door that sunny afternoon in August for a charged-up pastor. With enthusiasm and excitement in my voice I told Marge that I would like to serve her and Ralph Communion. Marge said she didn't know if he could manage the bread, but it was worth a try.

As I fumbled with the bread and grape juice in the kitchen, Marge tried to convey to Ralph what I wanted to do. From the kitchen I could hear Marge yelling to him, "She wants to serve you Communion!" Marge was still trying to get the message across when I entered the room with the bread and juice.

Now it was my turn to try and convey to Ralph what was going on. I joined in the yelling match, "Ralph, I want to serve you Communion . . . Communion . . . you know, the Lord's Supper!" To that Ralph said, "Corn supper . . . no . . . I don't want any corn."

Finally, with Marge's help, we were able to get him to understand that we were going to serve him bread and "wine." At that, Ralph smacked his lips and said, "I think I will have a little white wine."

Eventually Ralph received Communion. As I cleaned the little juice cups and washed the plate, Marge came into the kitchen. Since I was new at serving Communion, I didn't have a traveling Communion set. I had purchased small cans of grape juice for this day. The leftover juice was offered to Marge. She accepted with a sigh saying, "Maybe Ralph will drink this."

Wow! I had survived my first Communion! And what an experience! I looked back on that experience for weeks and had to chuckle at the comical sight Marge and I must have made as we yelled at Ralph. The whole neighborhood probably knew what was going on.

After that sunny day in August, I continued my weekly visits to Ralph's. It became apparent to me that he was more alert each time I visited. It even appeared that Ralph was putting on weight. It wasn't until the week before Thanksgiving that I noticed dramatic improvement in his physical and emotional well being. Marge said that she was so pleased with Ralph's improvement that she was sure that he would be joining her at the dinner table Thanksgiving Day.

I turned to Marge and asked, "What happened? When did Ralph begin to eat again?" Marge turned to me with tears in her eyes and said, "After you left that day you served Ralph and me Communion, I offered the leftover juice to him. That evening his appetite returned and he began to eat again and has been eating ever since."

We should never be amazed that God works in mysterious ways. But we are, aren't we? God used the symbols of bread and juice, representing Christ's body and blood, to touch and heal Ralph.

From One Trapeze

Vickie Dodge
Sullivan

What a joyful, challenging experience my Walk to Emmaus turned out to be. I had been a Christian for fifteen years before attending a Walk, and finally the big weekend was here. During a time of personal late night prayer, I heard God tell me I needed to quit my job. That might sound easy and even desirable if one were independently wealthy. However, the hard facts were that my husband was working two very part-time jobs, and I was trying to do photography out of our home, in addition to raising two small children and working at the University of Louisville. It was my U. of L. job that provided the bulk of our salary, our insurance and our security.

I was soon to discover that my source of security had been misplaced.

I came home from my Walk and shared the Lord's request with my husband, who supported me in this. But we both decided to wait until after a previously planned trip to Florida to see his parents. While in Florida the transmission went out on our van. The bill was just under

$2,000. We returned home, finished up our taxes, only to discover we owed $1,500 in self-employment Social Security taxes. Now our entire savings was gone, and I was supposed to quit my job.

I decided to make a deal with the Lord. "You provide Jeff (my husband) with a full-time job, with benefits, and then I'll quit my job," I bartered. I discovered he doesn't want to make deals. He wants obedience and faith. The image of a trapeze artist came to my mind. Like the woman on the trapeze who has to let go of one bar before reaching out to grab the other, I had to let go of the security my job represented and reach out to the Lord. He promised He would be the net for me and not let me fall.

With quiet confidence, and not a little anxiety, I gave my two week's notice at U. of L. That day when I got home, Jeff had received a call from our district superintendent (d.s.), offering him a full-time pastorate! One would think that with the timing and open door, I would have jumped with joy and praise. Anxiety, however, claimed my mind once again, as I thought of all the changes this would require. "We will have to move out of our own home. I'll have to move away from my mom! What will happen to my photography business?"

After a night of prayer, he told our d.s. "yes." We moved two months later. We were able to keep our home and rent it to another minister. We were only twenty minutes from my mother, and my photography business began to flourish. God is an awesome God! I am awe struck by his mercy, his patience and his goodness. During the five years we served our first church, he also blessed us with the desire of our hearts, two more children. Now we have what we always wanted, two boys and two girls. God is good all the time! All the time God is good!

Full Circle

Clarence LaMaster
Buck Creek

When I was very young, the evidence of my parents' faith in God was very apparent. At the age of five I knew this was how I wanted to live my life. I was baptized and dedicated my life to putting Him first in my life. I always had a blind faith that God would just always be there for me and my loved ones and carry us safely through whatever happened in our life. Jesus said "Whoever believed in me and has faith as a mustard seed needs only ask and it will be done for him."

God did carry us through some tough times and life seemed great! Then an awful sickness overcame Ella Mae, my wife and sweetheart of forty-eight years, and I asked God to please take the pain away and make her well. She, also, asked patiently for relief as did lots of our loved ones, but the pain kept getting worse until one night when she could tolerate it no more. Ella Mae got up and quietly walked away. She took a massive overdose of pills that had been meant to help her, but they did not do so.

All the while I had the faith that she would be well again, and this devastated my life and my faith was sorely tested. I was like a trusting child that had a promise from his father broken and is devastated! So there I was stumbling along, not knowing what had happened and just praying for answers. Then a truly wonderful person entered my life to guide me through.

Pastor Judy with her gentle, loving heart gently told me that all my prayers *were* answered but not in a way known to me, and that my Lord had kept his promises. Then another special Lady, Linda (aka Lolli the Clown) entered my life to help me gain courage and encouraged me to become a Smiles Unlimited Clown to put new joy in my life. So with even more encouragement from Pastor Judy I did just that, and I have had my life richly blessed by this experience. When I put on the face and clothing of Mr. Bo Jangles and can make children smile or put a smile on the face of someone who has lost all hope, I know that my Lord still has need of me, and life does indeed seen great once again! I have so many loved ones who truly care and want life to be great once again for me!

I feel now as if my life has come full circle, and once again I have that same trusting blind faith that I had as a small child of five years old. My faith was sorely tested and faith won! After an entire lifetime of following my Lord how could it possibly be any other way? Because He Lives, I can face tomorrow. With Faith to lead the way, tomorrow will be wonderful!

Husband, Son and Holy Light

Helen E. Elliott
Bryant

The testing of my faith first began when my son, Tom, became sick in January 1995. We thought it was pneumonia. However, on February 7, he was diagnosed as having lung cancer, which was not a result of smoking. Secondly, in March of that same year, my husband, Tom Sr., also became sick, which we initially thought to be the flu. However, in April the doctors told us that he, too, had cancer.

As the months wore on, both my son and husband received various chemotherapy and radiation treatments in an attempt to destroy the cancer. Our hopes were always high, but we all soon came to realize that a cure was not meant to be.

As the fall months approached, both men held onto their positive attitudes and outlook on life; however, their bodies were beginning to weaken. They both had experienced periods of time in and out of the hospital by the time November arrived. Tom Sr., my husband, was weakening quite a bit faster and by the beginning of December he was bedfast. My son's energy level had also rapidly become depleted. During this time, though, neither one complained about what was happening to their physical bodies; instead, they accepted the whole situation and knew their spiritual bodies were in God's hands.

On December 20, 1995, the Lord ended both their suffering, without the other knowing, within twenty-five minutes of each other. He had decided to bring them both to their eternal home to spend their first Christmas in heaven with Jesus.

It was early morning on December 20 after my son's family had left my house, and I was standing alone at my kitchen sink looking out my window, which faces east. It was still dark. As I gazed out the window, I saw the most brilliant, solid white circle of light. It was enormous. There was an image of my son on one side and my husband on the other. Then, it was gone. I knew right at that moment that God was showing me he had taken both my Tom's home together, and what a comforting thought to know. It really soothed my soul to know that God was taking care of them then, even as he daily cares for me until one day when I will meet my Toms again.

The Beauty of the Scars

Yung Sheng Chen
Indianapolis
(as told to Yvonne Thompson)

The nineteen-year-old prisoner tried talking to the captive next to him. He was frustrated from not knowing with whom he shared this torment.

The teen had been blindfolded with his hands tied behind his back for seven weeks. The thin mattress beneath him and deficient rice meals caused physical agony. Tired, terrified and confused, he was one of twenty-five people imprisoned in a small, basement burial room of this Buddhist temple.

Watching the crowded room, Chinese National soldiers caught the young prisoner trying to communicate with the other. As the guards approached, Yung Sheng Chen began to pray.

Yung Sheng, which means "everlasting life," had spent much of his incarceration in prayer. It was the spring of 1947 in Taiwan. Yung was well educated and a Christian, and had been falsely accused of having information about a revolt against the Chinese Nationals that had occurred in February. He was arrested at this mother's home on March 20. Yung missed her and his two brothers.

Talking was forbidden in the prisoner room. As the guards led Yung to a separate room, he didn't know if he would be beaten or shot. He did know once a prisoner left the room, that person rarely returned.

The backs and palms of Yung's hands were beaten. Each side was whipped fifty times. The soldiers then chained his bleeding hands behind his back before returning him to the prisoner room. Yung remained blindfolded, because his tormentors did not want him to see them.

One week later, the soldiers took Yung to an interrogation room in the middle of the night. Waiting outside the room the blindfolded Yung overheard someone else being verbally and physically battered. When it was his turn, Chinese Nationals questioned Yung's knowledge about the revolt. Answering an innocent "no" to the questions, two men simultaneously whipped his back. The torture lasted until early morning. Again, Yung had prayed for God to help him.

Another week passed, and Yung heard his name called by one of the prison officials. He thought if he underwent any more persecution, he would surely die. He prayed for grace to face it.

When interrogated again, Yung told his persecutors he was a Christian. He remembered the apostle Paul, and told them he was not afraid. He said if he had any information they wanted, he would tell them.

Six men struck him with baseball bats. Eventually, they forced him to kneel, beating him on the back until his head hit the ground. They also tried breaking his knees. The torture lasted two or three hours.

Following the beating, soldiers poked their pistols into Yung's chest twenty times, attempting to make him hemorrhage. They failed.

Knowing they wanted him to die, Yung endured more torture. A water hose was placed in Yung's mouth. As the rushing water filled his mouth, nose and ears, Yung collapsed, unconscious, before the water flooded his lungs. Still blindfolded, he was left for dead.

Within twenty-four hours, Yung regained consciousness. He thanked God that he still had life and that he could still pray. Scripture verses taught to him as a young child by his mother brought comfort, including 1 Thessalonians 5:17, which command believers to "pray without ceasing."

Yung prayed for two weeks as his body drifted between consciousness and near death. He was continually aware of "a sweet communion with Christ." He reached what he called "a sacred hour" where he reverently prayed for two things: to behold Christ and know God's plan for his life.

As he prayed to see Christ's face and hear his voice, Yung prepared to die if that was God's will.

Opening his eyes beneath the blindfold, Yung saw Jesus. Jesus was bright and pure, beautiful and holy, just as in the Transfiguration. Yung said he witnessed heaven, despite his prison hell.

Yung thanked Jesus for not despising him. He told him he was not worthy to have his prayers answered. He was frightened, but Jesus gave him peace by saying:

"Everlasting Life—you've been beaten, tortured and almost died. I'm going to call you and choose you as a divine vessel for the whole world. Do not be afraid. No one will ever touch you again. You belong to me. Wait for me nineteen more days. I shall return and get you out of this dungeon. Wait patiently for me."

Nineteen days later, Yung was released from prison. He had verbally shared Christ's love with the other prisoner, unharmed. After leaving, he prayed for God to heal his body, knowing his body was not his own. God gave him "divine strength," and he began working with foreign missionaries in Taiwan. He also attended seminary, and came to the United States in 1955 to study. He has been a United Methodist pastor for twenty-five years.

Yung has a scar on his left leg from the torture he survived, and calls it "the mark of Jesus." It keeps him humble and reminds him that God is faithful, watching over him wherever he goes. Whenever touching it, he says he can see where he has been, where he is and where he is going, and that Jesus Christ always remains the same.

When It Rains, It Pours

Rolla B. Hendrickson Jr.
Greensburg

I was forty-eight years old, in great physical shape, successful as a sales professional and active in the church. My lovely wife of over twenty-nine years and I were free to spend time together and make future plans for retirement and travel. However, we did anticipate more years of working and continuing in our accustomed lifestyle. Grown and married children were all healthy and beginning new lives. We studied the Bible, prayed, and sought God's direction in our lives. Suddenly it began!

Often we hear the expression "when it rains, it pours." The rains began and it did pour! The first downpour brought news that after being employed for over twenty-four years, I was losing my job due to downsizing efforts by my employer. Downpour number two was the decision of a son-in-law to leave his wife and three children, and bitter-sweet news that daughter and grandchildren needed to move in with parents. Almost two months later I received the diagnosis of colon cancer during a routine physical exam. Surgery was immediately scheduled for the day after Christmas, and sometime thereafter I began twelve months of rigorous chemotherapy. It was pouring! During this time I sought employment with no success.

Each day does indeed "have enough trouble of its own." Yet, when I finally realized that individual strength must be surrendered to God, the trials, troubles, and tribulation of this life became opportunities to hear God talk; to become sufficient in his strength alone.

Throughout the ordeals we have been blessed by the prayers and support given by family, friends and church family. My hospital stay and chemotherapy offered many opportunities to witness my faith in

Jesus Christ. Doctors, nurses, and other health care workers testified to me about their love for the Lord and his goodness.

At present, I fully understand neither the place nor the position God has prepared for us in this world. But health and stamina are returning. Our family is prospering. Although some have expressed admiration to us for the faith shown during difficult times, my intent is to offer a measure of support others who go through struggles. Know this! God will never leave you nor forsake you in this present life or in the life to come! Your trouble may be less or even greater than the ones described here. Bad things do happen to people. But I believe that God wants each of us to persevere. The Lord is full of compassion and mercy. To God be the glory!

Whispering Hope

Kathryne A. Foust
Kokomo

When our two beautiful twin girls were born two months premature they were both placed in incubators. They were each given too much oxygen which caused them both to be totally blind. Little did we know how heavy a responsibility was ahead of us. In later years we forced ourselves to face another problem of retardation. I felt like the bottom had fallen out of my world. This doesn't happen to me—other people not me. And what have I done in my lifetime to cause this to happen? I blamed myself for not having enough faith to heal our daughters. In my anger I blamed God.

Eleanor Roosevelt once said, "You gain strength, courage, and confidence by every experience in which you really stop to look fear in the face. You are able to say to yourself, 'I lived through this horror. I can take the next thing that comes along.' You must do the thing you think you cannot do." As our daughters went through eye surgeries, special care, special schools, and as my husband and I fought for the rights of our handicapped daughters, I held onto that quote. It uplifted me, it encouraged me, and I did do the things I had to do.

In later years we discovered the twins had a natural talent for music; this was a turning point for us. Our lives were filled with joyful song. They both performed many times in church and civic organizations. It was at one of these performances that a friend who had recently become a widow listened to our daughters sing "Whispering Hope." She decided if they could use their gifts then she, too, could still do something with her life. It wasn't until years later, as she related this story to us, we realized the twins did have a purpose here and that they were truly a blessing.

As we continue our journey, we look back and see laughter and tears, joy and sorrow, anger and healing. We can say we lived through this, we can take the next thing that comes along. We remember how God helped us through so many times and no matter what is ahead of us we will always have whispering hope.

Why Can't I Walk, God?

Michael Allen Prince
Mongo

Because I have quadriplegic cerebral palsy, I have to depend on somebody to help me with my personal needs. I used to think that I was almost like a tiny infant, and I tried to make something out of myself that I wasn't, to make me feel important. Way down deep in the pit of my soul, I had some regrets being born.

I have had many difficult questions for a young boy to have that no person knew the answers to, like "Why can't I walk, God? Why was I born to be a burden on my family? My God, why can't I take care of myself? I'm in the way, God; what did I do to deserve this handicap?"

Those questions were asked so many times with tears in my eyes. My God would bring me some sweet understanding. God knew the answers to my questioning, but I didn't know that then. I thought that God was punishing me, because I thought I did something wrong in God's eyes.

God hadn't forsaken me, although I felt like he had. My faith wasn't as strong then. I was beginning to doubt the Master's handiwork for my life. Most of the time, I had to watch the neighbors' children fly kites and play tag, from the cold metal confines of my wheelchair. In those times of heartache, longing to play those games with them, in my mind I felt so lonely, I would start to talk to God.

God was always sitting there beside me to feel my selfish pain, longing to be able to take care of myself. In those desperate times, God would send some kind miracle in my life to let me know that everything would be all right.

Miracles that I'm talking about are special friends who will stand by my side through every situation, friends that are so close to my heart they can relate to anything. Those dear friends and my strong-bonded family saved my heart from despair.

The way that I finally turned my self-pity into a rejoicing heart, I met someone I admire and love—Carolyn. When Carolyn was young, she had polio which left her unable to walk; and she rolled right into my life, as if God had placed her in my extended family.

While Carolyn was talking to me, she knew the turmoil I was going through, because she had those same questions after she had been struck with polio. She spent a couple of hours soothing my fears about my life with cerebral palsy, and she taught me so much in those precious few hours that she was here. Carolyn was sent by God to restore my hopes for my life; I still had my doubts about my life, but the doubts started fading away.

God uses people as messengers to help someone else through their tribulations and trials.

Today, I'm willing to follow Christ Jesus to the ends of the earth, witnessing to hurting people who might never have heard that Jesus loves them.

With God's wonderful kindness and overflowing mercy, I turned my life around from despair to victory. I wish I could spread God's love to everyone that has lost all hope in their lives and give them "Victory in Jesus."

Part Six

OUT OF THE DARKNESS

All the Promises

Harry H. Hashberger
Hagerstown

In August 1933 I attended Indian Springs Camp Meeting. The late Bishop Arthur J. Moore preached on Romans 12:1. "I beseech you therefore brethren by the mercies of God that you present your body a living sacrifice, holy, acceptable to God which is your reasonable service." That is what I did!

As a result of my total surrender to God's total control, the Holy Spirit directed me to Asbury College and Seminary. At that time I was a professional barber, making a little money, but nothing saved. The Holy Spirit led me to that so-dependable, rich promise of God in Philippians 4:19, "But my God shall supply all your needs according to his riches in glory by Christ Jesus." Now with my faith firmly fixed, I enrolled in Asbury College in September 1934, with my barber tools and exactly forty-five dollars. Several of us students "batched" to cut corners. I had to tighten my belt. Not that I went hungry, but obviously eating much less than when I was home.

True, it was rough going. At times I had two or three part-time jobs. Some of us fellows would try to build up a little morale with—"I came to college to work, not to get an education." I did campus work during the summers, mowing, etc. at twenty-five cents per hour. Thusly, I paid off my debt so I could enroll in the fall. Slowly but surely, I was

101

learning that all-important lesson. When God makes a promise, he expects us to do our part.

Goldie and I married in September '39 and were appointed to a two-point circuit. These dear people just did not have the money to pay the total salary of $400 from October 1 to June 1. But God supplied our needs, just as he said he would. He always has; he always will!

I retired, the second time, in June 1996. This September we will celebrate our fifty-ninth anniversary. Stop, look and listen! That is well over a half a century that we lived with that promise, tested it, proved it and have lacked no needs.

Some of you can remember with me the chorus "Every promise in the Book is mine." Indeed it is yours—and mine!

Changing the Course of a River

D. J. Cornelius
Brownsburg

One of the greatest gifts God has given each of us is the freedom of choice. We make millions of choices through the course of a lifetime. Like moving one large rock can change the course of a river over time, our choices can develop new channels for our life flow.

On the surface of my river of life the waters are calm; but like the deepest rivers, the current is not obvious. My life began like a waterfall, into a family in turmoil. In the small central Illinois community where I was born and spent most of my school years, I was a member of a prominent family.

The truth under the picture painted in public was a very dysfunctional family. Between the warring parents, sibling rivalries, alcoholism, and verbal abuse, I struggled to find an identity. For some of the family, church was an act of being seen in public and a deep facet of sanity for others. I found it to be a safe place.

For years I struggled with a quest for identity and escape. By the time I reached my senior year in high school, I realized my quest was to become whole. My guiding light to God through Christ was first revealed to me at church camp in southern Illinois.

It was our last night together. The weather was perfect, stars sparkling in the sky. I walked among my new friends to the open chapel for worship. We joined hands and sang "We are one in the Spirit, We are one in the Lord . . .," I started to realize that I had value to God and would some day be shown the way to make a difference in other people's lives.

After worship and Communion, we gathered in a circle around the fifteen-foot cross which is surrounded in a horseshoe by a brick wall. That night the cross seemed to glow in the blue moonlight. As we sang "Pass It On," I felt God enter my soul and begin to heal me.

As the morning sun rose, the melancholy feeling of fear began to return. Where would God be in the midst of the family turmoil I was about to return to? I wanted to run away rather than go back to being insignificant.

But God works in mysterious ways. As I finished high school my parents' world began to implode. The family business which Grandpa built had to be sold to settle a war between my dad and his brother. During my freshman year in college I looked everywhere but to God for escape. How could the God who sent his only son to save my soul allow so much pain in my life, my parents' lives, my sisters' lives?

Through the course of the next several years, I kept a weak devotion to my faith in God. As I redirected the flow of my life away from the restrictions of my prior experiences, I witnessed my parents lose everything. They risked the capital from a small community business venture, and lost everything.

Their loss turned out to be a significant turning point in my life. For the first time they allowed me to help make a difference in their future. Dad moved in with Eric, Erin, and me for several months.

Children lead many young adults back to the church. My "sunshine," Erin, was preschool age and I felt compelled to have her in Sunday School. Having been raised and confirmed Methodist, my quest for a church home was fairly well directed.

Gently the church, its ministers, and laypeople have brought guidance, growth, comfort, direction, peace, joy, hope and wholeness to my soul. The church has been the raft through many rapids in my river.

Through the United Methodist Church, God has transformed my life. Through faith in Christ's love and God's presence in my life, I have witnessed how God's gift of the freedom of choice makes a difference. I have consciously chosen to stop the cycles of abuse and co-dependence. I have chosen to equip my children to believe they are fabulous souls with a purpose in God's plan. Christ's message helps me to find the courage to paddle on toward the rapids when I reach the bend in my life's river.

This spring I traveled to Florida with my children, Eric and my mother. It was fabulous to share experiences with my children that I had as a child. I found that you can go back and rewrite memories. I now know to embrace the glorious childhood memories, learn from them, and let go of the rest.

I have found the strength to help make a difference in the lives of others. Like a rose in full bloom, I have become whole through the healing power of Christ. This process of redirecting the river has lead me to believing in the awesome power of God.

Come Home, My Son

Frank Wheeler
Lafayette

The best thing about becoming eighteen was leaving home and leaving the God of my youth. Leaving the judgmental, vindictive and unapproachable God I was required to "serve" several times each week. Leaving the relatively small town which constricted my actions. Leaving the familiar people whose very presence kept a fence around me. Leaving those things in search of freedom, a career, money, education—all those things which let Frank do just as he pleased.

Off to the anonymity of a large state university, the Army, first job and the allure of a bit of money and worldly success. Putting aside the occasional funeral and wedding, the church had no place in my life, God was a vague memory, Jesus irrelevant. Sometime in my early thirties I remember driving by a church being torn down and proudly proclaiming to my companion that it was the first time in five years that I had seen inside a church.

I also found the magic of alcohol—the answer for shyness, the remedy for disquiet, the balm for every hurt, the lubricant for every sticky problem. My best friend. A vital part of celebrating my marriage, sons' births, first promotion, new car; a way to deal with a death, mistake or concern. The answer for everything, good and bad.

But slowly, surely my best friend turned into my worst nightmare. My cherished freedom was lost in an insatiable, constant need for booze. I worked, I drank, I passed out every night. My wife was mother, father, gardener, everything necessary to try to hold the family together. Life became one long drunk—wild drives with our older son, shaky mornings, blurry nights, the family abandoned hundreds of miles away from home with only the clothes on their backs. Jail in Selma, Alabama on Easter morning 1980. Memories of trying to take my own life—desperation—my wife and brother there to pick me up.

A moment of clarity in a Nashville coffee shop: "Alcohol is killing me and those around me. How can I stop? Who can I turn to?" A few days later in a small orchard near an alcohol treatment facility, I knelt with my Dad and brother and prayed, "God, if you are there and you care, I need your help!" God was there and he cared.

I rose, a certain peace came over me which has not left to this day. I embraced the recovery program and in the Tennessee hills one spring nearly twenty years ago, I found God. Not the angry God of my youth but a loving, caring, approachable God, a "very present help." A God who opened his arms to say, "Son, come home." A God who did not say first join a church, tithe, do this, don't do that. But a God who just said, "Son, come home."

And I did. A Methodist church and its minister which had become an anchor for my wife also became so for me. My first Sunday back from rehabilitation was Mother's Day and Mildred called to inform me I was taking her to church, the first Mother's Day for her to attend since her own son's death many years before. We walked in—me self conscious, but Mildred holding my arm and proudly marching up front. Most important of all, a wife and two sons willing to say, "Dad, come home."

Along the way I met this fellow, Jesus, dealt with much of the wreckage of my past, learned generally to live with a certainty, serenity, and faith. Dealt with the highs and lows of life without the need for alcohol, started learning a bit about what love means, found friends and looked at God's world through new eyes. Not perfect, not always loving, not always happy, but sober, willing to learn and grow, and mostly calm—all because God simply but clearly said, "Come Home, my son."

Faith x 3 = 6

Morris Conly
Fort Wayne
(as told to Minietta Millard)

In the early 1950s Harriet and Morris Conly's lives were on a joyful and fulfilling path as Morris accepted a job change and Harriet discovered she was pregnant again. Their lives with two sons, Dan (four) and Michael (five), were centered around church activities and their faith in God.

As Harriet's pregnancy advanced, doctors discovered she was expecting triplets. The babies continued to grow, but she began to lose weight and was eventually hospitalized.

This was before fertility drugs, so there was much excitement and interest among the hospital staff. In the eighth month, three doctors assisted in the delivery of Tim, Sally and Emily. The babies did well, but Harriet was put in an oxygen tent. Doctors were puzzled about the cause of the complications but thought she may have had an aneurysm; the end result was that she was not expected to live through the night. She died about three days later of static pneumonia.

Morris attended church the first Sunday after Harriet's death; he took a stance that "we have to believe and go for it." This seemed to give church members courage, and they rallied around with support and strength. Executives at his job asked Morris what they could do. He replied, "Give me a job with more pay," and they did. Even with this enormous amount of reinforcement, the devastating event of his wife's death kept Morris physically cold for over a year.

Morris never once considered giving up his five children. Instead, he trusted in God to send him a housekeeper/nanny who came in the form of a fine, loving, Christian woman who helped raise the children for many years.

Eventually when the triplets were eight years old, Morris met Marjorie through the minister's association and they were later married. It took a huge amount of faith on her part to step into this family of five young children and later even give birth to one more, Frank, to expand the crowded household.

Looking back Morris says, "It all just worked out." It was not a time to stand around and wonder why, it was a time to believe that God is in charge and a time to do whatever needed to be done—one step at a time.

Falling into Grace

Jeff Marshall
Mishawaka

January 3, 1997—a day that will forever remain etched in my memory, the day I hit "bottom" with my addiction. My wife, Gail, came home from work with evidence of my addiction, and asked me to leave our home after nineteen years of marriage. Following that confrontation, I faced my five children with the truth about my secret life, went to my district superintendent, resigned as pastor of my church and surrendered my credentials as elder in the Conference, then went to tell my parents, brother and sisters about my addiction.

I felt as if my life was over and that I would be severely shunned by everyone I knew. That is the terrible lie one lives with in an addiction:

"I am no good! Nobody would love me if they knew the truth!" What I expected to face in the future was a life of isolation. I was not prepared for the response from family and friends.

For twenty-five years I lived believing that I was unacceptable, even to God, because of the life of sin in an addiction. I did everything I could to earn love from others, even from God. I spent almost seventeen years in ministry preaching about the grace and love of God, but I never really fully experienced that grace and love in my own life.

At nine years of age I accepted Jesus Christ as my Savior and began growing as a child of God. But later that growth was hampered by bondage to an addiction, and I chose to ignore the words of the apostle Paul in Ephesians 2: "For it is by grace you have been saved, through faith—and this not from yourselves, it is the gift of God—not by works."

When I thought I could not experience God's grace, He sent grace through a mother and father, sisters and a brother, through Ron and Susan, Tom and Janet, Kelvin and Kathy, Jeff and Debbie, Ted and Jenny, Dave and Roberta, Donald and Beth, Charles and Paula, Tim, John, Ted, Doug, Woody, Carolyn, Gene and Jeanie, Barbara, Don and Betty, Bob and Peg, Marietta, Winslow and Linda, Chuck, Fred and Sandy, Dorothy, Bob, Jane, Jim and Yvonne, Carl and Peg, John and Joann, Don, Mark, Nimbi, Woody, Cindy, Jack, Dick and Karen, Mary, Fran and Orville, and yes, through a wife's undying love and with five children who chose to love in spite of the hurt and pain caused by a husband's and father's addiction.

When I could not experience God's grace, the church brought that grace to me. Over the next few months I came to experience that grace directly from a loving God who reached down into my heart and continued the work of transformation and sanctification that was begun when I accepted Jesus into that heart as a child.

On January 3, 1997, I fell into grace as the people of God lifted me into the loving arms of my heavenly Father.

God and Good Business

Dawn Jarvis
Kokomo

In 1986 I ventured into my own business. After having twenty-eight years of experience as a dispensing optician, I felt confident I could continue on my own. Boy what a learning experience! Four months after we opened our business, the bottom (I thought) fell out from under us. The money that we had to invest in our business didn't last long. I thought I did it all right—I paid for everything as we went, and four months later the cash flow was exhausted. That is when I told my husband we would have to leave town because our pride would not allow us to face the public, friends, and relatives as failing in business. We sold an old truck for $700 and borrowed money from credit cards to try to stay above water. After several months of weary life, I fell to my knees, cried, prayed, and had to believe God would make us a success.

He sent people to our office in this stressful time. Some came to pray and one lady even shared with me that the devil had taken over and I needed to get him out. She prayed and cried with me. I believe God sent her as well as others to pray with me and to encourage me.

Years later, again feeling like a failure, I had a faithful experience. We had just hired a doctor and moved into our present location. For three days very few people came through our door. Again I felt weak and called upon the Lord to lift me up out of despair. On this particular day I resorted to my quiet office, prayed, and read my scripture. Between 3:00 and 7:00 P.M. I had nineteen new clients walk into my office. God led them to me, caused me to stay overtime, and he said to me "Dawn, you continue to test me; won't you please have faith and believe in yourself too." To this day I don't test him and when I stay faithful in my prayer and scripture, the Lord truly blesses our business.

I also had a healing on my back one particular Sunday. The elders were anointing a small girl with leukemia and one of the elders came to me and said you know you can come here too. I told him it's not for me to be healed but for the girl. He had walked away and after some thought (maybe if I only touched the hem of the robe), I went to the altar believing that I must be healed. I cannot face another back surgery. During the prayer of healing my back became very hot and I walked away with no pain.

The Lord is awesome and I pray the lost souls will soon reach up for the Lord before it is too late.

Leaving Is Not an Option

Anna Marie Fernihough
Jeffersonville

Faith for a disabled person is one of the most difficult concepts to grab hold of, but at the same time, it is the most essential element of life. Faith is the difference between accepting one's limitations and continuing to live, and feeling sorry for oneself and losing everything.

I have been told that 96 percent of multiple sclerosis patients get divorced. Most people feel sorry for the patient and blame the spouse for being unable to cope. Maybe for some, this is true. But I wonder how many patients cause the problems. MS isn't easy to live with. It is a disease that changes, sometimes within seconds. Many patients and families live with the daily fear of complete incapacity.

In 1988, six weeks before my husband was to graduate from the University of Akron, on the day of an algebra final, I was told that I had MS.

People, including family on both sides, had the audacity to ask my husband of eleven years at that time, when he was going to leave me.

Angrily, resentfully, he told them in no uncertain terms that leaving was not an option. They still, after nine years, wonder why.

But it's not that hard. We both have faith. First in God, then in each other.

Frustration? Much more that we deserve. Anger? More than we can put into words.

But we have God. What more do we need?

Lower Lights Burning

Walter Mayer
Bringhurst

"Let the Lower Lights Be Burning," a hymn conspicuous by its absence in the new hymnal, was composed as the result of a shipwreck near the harbor in Cleveland, Ohio. During a ferocious night storm on Lake Erie, the lighthouse beacon failed to function and, as a result, the pilot missed the channel and struck the shoals. The ship sank almost immediately taking many lives to the bottom—a national disaster, as it was reported. Dwight L. Moody, the great evangelist, was later to say in one of his sermons that "God will keep the heavenly lights burning. That's his job. Our task is to keep the lower lights burning." "Some poor fainting, struggling seaman you may rescue, you may save."

Although I had sung that old hymn since childhood, its potential was never revealed until a midnight experience deep into the Canadian wilderness not so many years ago.

Along with our fishing companions of twenty years, Bob and Phyllis, we had for some reason stayed up unusually late singing hymns by the light of a Coleman lantern. Well on toward midnight we had come to our favorite hymn and had just finished the chorus, "send a gleam across the wave," when we heard the faint cry from out on the lake, "Help! Please help us!" We were the only campers in the region and a light snow was falling already in September.

We grabbed our lantern and ran down to the dock to find three men in a small boat with no idea where they were. Normally, only bear hunters would be coming in and those with a seasoned guide.

Their gas supply was nearly exhausted along with their food. For whatever reason, their pilot had not returned to pick them up on the designated day. Unwisely, they abandoned their campsite following the lakeshore around endless bays and islands, often curling back on themselves, desperately trying to find some evidence of human life in the dark.

Had our small lantern not been shining, they would have passed us in the night with nothing ahead of them. We were it! A late night choir practice in the darkness. That was the night my childhood hymn came alive and in the most unlikely place. In that flash point I knew there is no such thing as coincidence. Never again! Later I was to remember Paul and Silas singing hymns from their prison cell at midnight unaware who might be listening down the corridor and crying out "What must we do to be saved?"

I Once Was Lost

Roberto Suarez Rivas
Indianapolis

As I leave this place that I have come to call home, it is my deepest wish to express how I discovered my newfound faith.

Very simply put, when I found myself in so much pain and wanted to die, I fell to my knees and cried out, "Dear Lord, please take away the pain." I now understand that things happen for a reason. When going through the needed pain of change, that this process of recovery brings, it is then that the spirit grows stronger and more courageous. Through a willingness to believe in God, I am now confident I posses the heart to grab life by the throat and make it relinquish the joy and peace God has promised.

Life and addiction can be formidable enemies, but I believe faith is greater. One nurtures faith one day at a time, so do not be discouraged. I came into Raines a fearful child; I now leave as a man of good faith and character. Within this letter I leave my faith and hope that your lives will have peace and joy. The same peace and joy I have found while living here at Lucille Raines.

(The Lucille Raines Residence is a United Methodist-related social service agency.)

One True Friend

Danny Kay Lung Sr.
Muncie

As a small child I was physically abused by my adopted father. For example, I had been tied to the front tree and chained to the back clothesline. Or sometimes when things were real bad, a leather whip was used. This went on for several years.

When I was nine years old I started to work at a place called Pine Manor. After a couple of weeks I met a boy and we became good friends. Later on he asked me over to his clubhouse. When we got there, he introduced me to his family. They called themselves the Bandinos. Shortly after this I, too, became a member of the family. Eight years and 1,900 cuts, stitches, stabs, and gunshot wounds later, a police officer came to me and said that I had better think of joining the service or I'd be joining my friend in prison.

So after thinking about my future, I decided to join the service. So, in July 1969 I joined the United States Marine Corps. During my time in the Corps I was taught how to kill, how to protect myself, but most of all how to have pride in myself. During this time I met two new friends. And they stayed my friends until I was twenty-eight years old. Their names were drugs and booze.

After two years of Vietnam I was discharged and sent home. By then I was becoming a very hardened person. By the time I got home, people started to spit on me and calling me a baby killer. After a month of this, I completely hated the world and everyone in it.

About a year later I met this young lady and things started to look up for me. She loved me for who I was, and I truly loved her.

We got married on April 24, 1971. Shortly thereafter we had our first son. For the first time I felt like I really was someone. But once again it did not last long. My two friends were back stronger than ever. One day after being on a two-day party I took a gun and tried to kill the two most important people in my life. Needless to say, I did not complete what I had started.

Years later fate turned on me again. Tom, our newborn son, came down with spinal meningitis. The doctors only gave him a 10 percent chance to live. As I stood there looking at him—helpless, unable to help him—I looked at my hands. The hands that kept me from harm for years were now useless. Well, someone was looking out for Tom that day because he's now fourteen years old and doing well.

Months later a friend of the family came over. He said he had something to share with me and my family. If I knew then what it was all about I would have not let him in the door. He started to share what God had done in his life. Then he kept asking us to church. I got so tired of hearing about it that I said yes just to shut him up.

Well the next Sunday we went and there I met a man that changed my life around. His name was Jesus. He did not do anything great (no feats of magic or miracles). All he said was that he loved me. He loved me for who I was. That day I gave my heart to him, and I'll never be the same again.

Pumpkin Pie Memories

Dianne McAlpin Walker
New Paris

Throughout our seven years of ministry and marriage, there have been mountaintops and valleys. In the summer of 1994 I was hospitalized for four months. I wasn't sure if I was going to live or whether I had anything to live for. When I discovered that we couldn't have children, I felt cheated and that I was disappointing my husband. Feeling led by God, we turned to being foster parents. It seems that whenever things were a bit challenging at the church our foster children were there with a hug and a smile.

My husband and I have fostered fifteen children in the past three years. We will always remember our first set of foster children. Michael and Raymond were brothers. Michael was four years old and Raymond who we called Ray-Ray was eighteen months old. They lived in our home from the first of November until Christmas Eve when they returned home.

Ray-Ray loved pumpkin pie. We have a special picture of my husband holding Ray-Ray on his lap while they shared a piece of Thanksgiving pumpkin pie loaded with lots of whipped cream. Ray-Ray loved playing the piano, enjoyed music and always had a smile on his face. Michael enjoyed helping me in the kitchen. He especially liked to help bake cookies. One night we took Michael for a walk past the church. It was Christmas time and a manger scene was set-up in front of the church. Michael began to ask questions about the crèche. Tears came to my husband's eyes as he explained the Christmas story to a four-year-old who acted as if he had never heard it before in his life.

Their departure came too soon for us. By Christmas Eve they had returned to live with their mother. We continued to keep in touch with them and their family. Our last time seeing Ray-Ray and Michael together was the weekend before Easter 1995. They stayed all weekend with us, searched for Easter eggs in our yard, went to the circus, and we celebrated Ray-Ray's second birthday. Before leaving, his face covered with frosting, he gave me a big hug and said "I love you and can't wait to see you again."

That was the last time we saw Ray-Ray alive. Shortly after, he admitted to Riley Children's Hospital via helicopter. When we went to see him, it was too late. While I was buying balloons in the gift shop my husband went to the desk to get Ray-Ray's room number. There he was informed that Ray-Ray had died. A boyfriend of the mother had shaken and beaten him to death.

We loved Ray-Ray like he was our own son. There were so many questions, and the pain we shared was unbearable. We nearly gave up being foster parents. Yet there was something that kept us going. There are times you feel called and continue despite all the unpleasant and dreadful circumstances. Somehow we continued, with our love and faith in each other.

We are glad and rejoice in how God gave us the strength to continue. Thirteen children later we still have our moments, yet the joys of loving a child in need surpasses all the pain. Today we have a sixteen-year old girl that wants to live with us for life and a two-year-old boy that one day we hope to adopt, plus two sisters age eleven and eight. What matters the most in our lives is that fifty years from now there will be an adult that can have memories about living in a foster home where their foster mom and dad loved them. We all need to remember "Children are a gift from God." We need to love, not judge.

The one thing I've learned through all the pain and suffering is that when horrible things happen they are followed by blessings. It's difficult to say and hard to believe but the suffering times should be a time of praise for the blessings that will follow.

The Last Bell

Harold Leininger
Brownsburg

What is irreconcilable for human beings is reconcilable through the power of God. This truth came to me in an unforeseen but concrete way while we were visiting in Rostov, a city of one-and-a-half million people in the Ukraine. Early in the morning before breakfast, I took a walk into a poor section of the city. I saw two young girls in uniform running down the street in front of me and then turning a corner. Out of curiosity I decided to follow them. I saw them enter a narrow opening into a large brick walled courtyard. Approaching the opening, I saw a great gathering of people. There were children who appeared to be first graders reaching up to possibly ninth graders standing in a large rectangle with their parents behind them. On one side were the school officials and other dignitaries. I asked if there was a translator. Several persons scurried around through the faculty to find an interpreter.

Finally, a young man came and explained in broken English that this was graduation day. I introduced myself by saying I had come to the Soviet Union on a pilgrimage on behalf of peace. The young man left to get the director of the school and the Soviet official in charge. They quickly came to me and took me to a place of honor where all the dignitaries were seated.

With nearly 400 in attendance, the Soviet party official presented me with a dozen red carnations. The ceremony in progress was interrupted. I was introduced to the joyful crowd as an American visiting the Soviet Union. I moved to the microphone. I told those gathered, "I have come in prayer from the United States on a mission of peace. I have children your ages (grades one through nine). More than anything, my children want peace not war. They want you not as enemies but as friends, so together they may have with you many many years of peace." At the close of my brief speech, I invited all present to come to Indianapolis and visit us. A whoop came up through the crowd. I then urged them to be in prayer with me that General Secretary Mikhail Gorbachev and President Ronald Reagan (who was landing that morning in Moscow) might bring the world new dimensions of peace.

As I finished speaking, the graduating class of students spontaneously broke away from the crowd. They ran across the courtyard to me and gave me bouquets of flowers they had brought to give to their favorite teachers. The flowers became so many I could not hold them all in my arms. The officer took the flowers from me and asked me to be seated for the rest of the ceremony. Quietly without a sound the eighth grade class of graduates marched out of the courtyard. Suddenly a father came forward. He put his first-grade child on his shoulders and gave her a giant bell. The little child bouncing on her father's shoulders rang the bell vigorously while he ran around the courtyard in front of all the people. The child was ringing the last bell of school. The party officials embraced me with bear hugs. Another school official took pictures with those gathered around me. With everyone still standing, I spoke these words over the sound system, "The last bell must be the bell for peace!"

Waving good-bye, I invited the party official and the school director to accompany me back to my hotel. Graciously, the two men carried all of my flowers as we walked down the streets of Rostov. When we arrived, my tour group had finished breakfast. My wife, Andrea, had been ready to call the authorities to find out where I was. I introduced the two men to all present, and a lively discussion followed. Afterwards we boarded the bus in front of the hotel in order to go to Leningrad. We said our final good-byes. The Communist Party official embraced me once again with tears clearly glistening in his eyes. He watched our bus leave until we were out of sight. I knew then the last bell was, indeed, the bell for peace.

Wrapped in Love

Esther J. Thompson
Mishawaka

"My God, my God, why have you forsaken me?" (Matthew 27:46). These words leaped from the page as I studied my Lenten devotional. Now I understood that was the silent cry I had uttered when I was told that my precious daughters were in a fatal automobile accident on the way to school!

I could still see my husband, Jack, pacing the sidewalk as I drove in front of the house. His words still echo in my ears, "Sharon is dead! Our beautiful daughter is gone! So is her friend, Tony. Cathy is being Life-Lined to Methodist Hospital with our neighbor, Tammy. They give them a fifty-fifty chance of making it."

My scream of pain and disbelief echoed through the air. I felt abandoned and alone. Family and friends were all around me, yet I felt like I was isolated on an island, out of contact with God and all my loved ones. My world had fallen apart. This was truly the Good Friday in my life.

After the funeral, I threw all my energy into helping Cathy mend. Her determination provided the strength to get through the days, but memories haunted me.

Several months later, I was lying on my bed crying when I heard Sharon calling, "Mom, Mom, don't cry. I'm alright."

There was a warm, bright light radiating from the corner of the room where her voice came from. Suddenly I felt like someone had wrapped me in a blanket of comfort and love. I knew I was no longer alone. I fell to my knees and held out my hands to God and prayed, "Lord, thank you for the sixteen wonderful years I had this beautiful child. Now I know she wants to be with you and now I must surrender her to you."

As I rose from my knees, I knew that I was no longer alone. The Lord was with me, and the healing process began.

Part Seven

MOMENTS OF HOLY BEAUTY

A Heart for Glass

Minnietta Millard
Indianapolis

Career counseling had shown decisively that I was experiencing burnout working on a church staff, because my heart was beating the song of an artist. This was difficult for my pastor husband to accept because his vision was the two of us together on a staff "forever and ever. . . ."

Over the months to come I gave the situation to God again and again. Do I shatter his dream? Do I respect my needs? Do I dare risk the unknown of a new direction?

God, in God's time, answered: "Follow the passion of your heart; I will be with you."

With that decision made, another waiting began concerning which medium to pursue. Reading the paper one day, I saw a picture of a woman working in colored glass. I can only explain what happened as a bolt of lightning hitting me with a "knowing."

I immediately took a class in leaded glass and resigned my job at the church two days later. The "knowing" could only have been from God because it is the perfect medium for me artistically and spiritually.

In the midst of life's struggles, God is faithful. And sometimes the answer is a knowing beyond all human knowledge, which can be trusted completely.

Amid Soldiers & Hymns

Joe Wagner
Colfax

I had been invited to Liberia in December 1995 to attend a planning conference for the Liberia Annual Conference of the United Methodist Church. One morning, during the conference, Bishop Arthur Kulah was sharing his experience of his recent trip to Ganta. Since the church has a school and a hospital at Ganta, I asked about the possibility that I might go there after the conference had concluded. He replied, "No problem; we will go." He later related some of the difficulties he had in getting there because of the military checkpoints, and I began to wonder if I had made the right decision. The missionary couple I was with thought I was crazy for even considering the trip. I could still change my mind . . . and almost did. A couple of days later Bishop Kulah announced that the plans were settled; we were going to leave on Friday.

On Friday morning we gathered at the conference center. The night before, a group of refugees had been transported to Monrovia and to the conference center, en route to their home villages. Many had been away from their homes for four or five years. As they prepared to board the United Methodist Committee on Relief truck that morning, taking all their possessions which they could carry on their heads, and as we prepared to leave for our 200-mile trip to Ganta, Bishop Kulah called us all together and led us in a rousing stanza and chorus of "My Hope Is Built On Nothing Less." Here we all were, on the brink of a journey, facing the unknown and together claiming and affirming the promise of God. Then Reverend Levi Williams prayed for God's protection and peace to be with us all. At that moment I felt assured that God would protect us.

After stopping to get bottled water, bread, and money, we started on our journey to Ganta. We left Monrovia and drove for miles seeing only empty shells of houses and churches in the midst of weeds, trees, and shrubs. I was saddened as I thought, "The homes of the refugees will probably look like these."

The first fifty miles were in control of the West African peace keepers. So far, so good. However, at that point we entered the area controlled by rebel leader Charles Taylor. There we experienced many checkpoints occupied by twelve- to sixteen-year-old soldiers. Ragged jeans and T-shirts were their uniforms. Some of the guns were larger than those who were carrying them.

When we reached Gbarnga, about three quarters of the way to Ganta, I wanted to visit Tubman-Gray, an Operation Classroom mission school. The Bishop intended that we visit the seminary campus as well. As we approached the seminary there was a checkpoint guarded by three young soldiers. The Bishop and the young soldiers began to argue about the checkpoint gate. The Bishop said the check-point was to have been removed. They continued to argue, when one of the teenagers walked over and picked up his gun and came back to the car. My heart quickened as I wondered what would happen next. The Bishop made some statements about the inappropriateness of drawing a weapon on a civilian, while we sat anxiously wishing he would stop arguing. Finally, we were allowed to pass the checkpoint. We heaved a collective sigh of relief as we visited the seminary and school campuses.

We continued our journey to Ganta, arriving around 4:30 P.M. and settled into our rooms, furnished only with old mattresses. On Saturday we visited the hospital, the leper colony, and the school. At the leper colony we had a worship service. One man prayed, "God, I thank you that I saw the sun come up this morning and I pray I will be able to see it go down this evening." It was an experience of introspection as I sat and listened to these people who have experienced so much adversity sing and express their faith. That evening the young people of the church had a welcoming ceremony for us. However, we had to wait until they got fuel for the generator. The resulting lights were dim and it was nearly impossible to read the hymnals, but we were grateful for the light and I was thankful that I knew the hymns. The choir sang several songs, including "God Is Not Dead." They praised God in the midst of being displaced. They expressed a hope that God, in his time, would bring peace to their land. As I lay on my mattress on the floor that night, I prayed and recommitted myself to the work we were doing in Liberia.

On Sunday we had a meaningful Communion service with the displaced who were staying at Ganta. We gratefully ate a bowl of rice and a tough piece of chicken before we left for the journey back to Monrovia. The checkpoints were not a problem and we arrived before dark. My faith had grown. I had experienced faith in others' lives in a way I had never experienced before.

Assurance Alive!

Anita Owen Fenstermacher
South Bend

All of us are gathered for a family cookout celebrating my parents', brother and sisters' visit. We are having a great time when we hear someone up the street crying hysterically. My mother hears the screaming continue and turns to my brother, David, who is a pastor and says, "Go see if you can help that person." I am praying for David's wisdom when Mom turns to me and says, "You're a missionary, go with him." As we walk up the street, I pray for spiritual discernment for us both.

A crowd is gathered at a home and people are trying to calm a teenage girl who is hysterical. She has been alone with her ill mother as she died in her arms. No one can break through the hysteria. I turn her toward my face and say firmly but lovingly, "Stop it! Your mother isn't dead!" The hysteria stops and, as I hold her, she listens as I share the faith in the resurrection on which I stake my life.

Little did I know that less than twenty-four hours later I would be riding in an ambulance to the Harrisburg Hospital. In the rear of the ambulance is my dead three-and-a-half year old son, Eric, and a critically injured mother. As I hold my injured nine-month-old daughter, Heidi, on my lap, the driver keeps saying, "Now, lady, just try to stay calm!" He couldn't know that I am repeating to myself all I had said the day before to the teenager about the faith on which I stake my life.

Many comments are made to me—some helpful and some distressful from a faith perspective. But when my husband Bob and I are finally able to share, we each have had the experience of Christ holding us in his arms, sobbing with us as our hearts are breaking. I know that when I see Eric in the casket, I am so aware that his vibrant spirit is somewhere else.

It is hard to return to our pew in worship. We sit in the balcony where Eric often fell asleep with his head on our laps before church was over. My lap is so empty!

But the next Easter, a miracle occurs during worship. The birds are singing in the budding trees outside the opened balcony windows, and we all stand to sing, "Up from the grave He arose, with a mighty triumph o'er his foes." Growing up in church, I cannot remember the first time I heard that hymn. It is a part of my psyche.

While that hymn is sung, my spirit leaves that place. Words are inadequate, but somehow I am lifted out of time and space and I meet Christ. Eric is with him and I am there. I know we are one forever. Easter is real and assurance alive. An assurance on which I stake my life.

A Bouquet of Trust

Minnietta Millard
Indianapolis

The leader of the workshop was a powerful, focused woman who had long ago committed her life to a "very loving God"; I was a member of her volunteer staff. We had worked as a sacrificial, loving team to bring about transformation in the lives of the participants, and now it was time to celebrate with a splendid banquet.

Each of the staff was given an assignment to accomplish in the brief three hours before the event: some were to purchase the food, some were to arrange for decorations. Jan and I were to locate a gorgeous bouquet of flowers "through faith." In other words, we could spend no money; it was an experience of "ask and you shall receive" in the center of a booming city.

I never lost faith and focused every moment on the task. I found the courage to ask again and again. Sometimes people were supportive and friendly; at other times I was given a cold shoulder and looks of suspicion. Finally I found an office that would loan us flowers for the evening. When I reported back to workshop headquarters, I discovered that the bouquet was to be given away at the banquet so a loan wouldn't work. I made a mental note: know exactly what you need before you ask.

As the time limit ticked away, I kept calm and determined and carried a prayer in my heart that God would guide us. Minutes before the deadline, I returned to our room empty handed just in time to see a tearfully overwhelmed Jan enter the room with an enormous bouquet of magnificent flowers of every color!

Jan had been out in the streets asking florists or any potential donor. Just as she was about to give up, she saw a man to whom she had responded compassionately when his family was in need; she could barely recognize him behind a huge bouquet of flowers. When she shared her mission, he handed the flowers to her with no hesitation; he felt honored to be able to repay her for her kindness.

This experience has been a model for my life. Whenever I want to make a difference in the world, I set a definite goal, turn it over to God, work as though it all depended on me, and trust—knowing it all really depends on God.

And God has been faithful to this day.

Bringing Church

Andrea Leininger
Brownsburg

Several months ago Jane came to Calvary Church for the first time. Following the service, she leaned over to her sister Marcia and said, "This is the church!" Then and there Jane, Marcia, and brother-in-law Milo decided they wanted to be members of our congregation.

Several times I invited Jane to the Newcomer Class, but she wasn't able to attend. Why? She discovered she had cancer. Chemotherapy treatments wore her out, and then she had to deal with all the back pain. But Jane and I chatted by phone regularly.

A couple weeks ago Jane was rushed to Methodist Hospital. CAT Scan reports revealed that the cancer had spread to her lungs, bladder and heart. She was given only a few days to live. I spent about five hours with Jane and her family. I asked her if she still wanted to join our church. She said, "Yes, it's very important!" So, I asked her a membership question: "Do you confess Jesus Christ as your Lord and Savior?" "Oh, yes," she declared. "Jane, you're now a member of Calvary Church!" Then she fell back to sleep.

A couple days later she asked if I would hold a church service for her family, since she knew she would never be back with us here at Calvary. I took the challenge. I asked about all her favorites—music, singers, scripture, stories, etc. Then I designed a special service just for them. On a Sunday afternoon in the Hospice Unit at Methodist, twelve of us gathered. Jane was having a good day. We sang "Amazing Grace" and "How Great Thou Art." A couple of nurses and strangers from the next room came in and joined us. Then, Jane's daughter-in-law and son sang a duet with guitar. During our "Sharing Our Reflections" time, I listened to a family tell each other how much they loved one another. Both her son and daughter thanked their mother for leading them to Jesus Christ. Jane talked about what a privilege it was to know she would soon enter heaven with Jesus. I felt so blessed to be an intimate part of this family sharing.

Then Jane looked to me and said, "Andrea, I am so glad God brought me to your church. You are all so friendly and caring. But the main reason I came was because in your church, I saw Jesus." She thanked me for allowing her to become a member from her bed. I was humbled by her rich faith both in God and in us.

As we offered words and hugs of peace and love to each other, I knew I had been to "church." For in that hospice room packed with family, friends, and a few strangers, I saw Jesus. I wept as I came down the corridor to the back door of the hospital. I breathed a prayer to God, "Lord, I just wish the whole church could have been with us today."

Every Common Bush Afire

Susan W. N. Ruach
Bloomington

Although this event happened several years ago, it is still meaningful to me. One night I had a dream—a snippet of a dream really—in which I saw a calendar page for January 19, and a voice said, "Watch it!" Now, I believe many dreams come from God, so I made a note in my calendar on January 19 to "Watch it"—to be careful.

Given my busy schedule on the days around the nineteenth, I decided to take that day off—especially since my children only had a half day of school that day. However, in the shifting of other commitments, I somewhat reluctantly agreed to do an evening workshop in the town where my parents lived, a hundred and twenty-five miles away.

As the nineteenth drew nearer, I wasn't quite sure how to approach it. I did finally ask a friend to pray for me. Then the nineteenth arrived. During a quiet moment in the morning, the thought flitted through my mind that if something catastrophic happened, I might not "be here" tomorrow. It didn't feel morbid—more matter of fact.

That afternoon as I related to my kids, I found myself being more patient than usual about things that I usually would have complained about. At one point I looked at my thirteen year old—an ordinary sort of thirteen year old whom I see every day—and I was struck by the realization that he was really an incredible human being.

Midafternoon my son, my ten-year-old daughter and I got into the car to drive the roads we frequently travel to my parents, where I'd leave the kids and then go on to the workshop. My daughter fell asleep in the front seat; and, as I looked over at her, a sense of awe came over me at who she was.

It rained most of the way. Sometimes it was steady and soft; sometimes, a heavy downpour. The red-brown grass glistening in the rain and against the dark brown earth was incredibly beautiful. The clouds in various shades of gray rolled and tumbled and tussled with each other in almost incandescent splendor as they were blown across the sky. A little farther along, the black, leafless trees in exquisite silhouette stood out against the sky. Each scene along that very familiar way glistened and vibrated with incredible beauty. Mile after mile passed with varied and luminescent scenes, all of them equally beautiful.

Later at the workshop, I saw the people through eyes of wonder at their willingness to take three hours at the end of a long day to learn to better teach the faith that sustained them. This was no ordinary group of teachers—or was it?

On the twentieth, the "danger" past, I wondered about my dream and my interpretation of it. What did it really mean? And in the wondering, the gift it gave me became clear: the enhanced day, the perception of beauty always available, the awesomeness of people through the eyes of love. I remembered Elizabeth Barrett Browning's poem:

> Earth's crammed with heaven,
> and every common bush afire with God;
> But only . . . (those) who see, take off . . . (their) shoes—
> The rest sit around it and pluck blackberries . . .
> (Sonnets from the Portuguese, VII, 1.820)

If only I could "see" more often. If only we all could "see" all the time.

Hill Country Pieta

Jill Williams
Bloomington

The road went from blacktop to gravel to dirt ruts. The spring sun reflected off a creek, dancing along the roadside ditch and took the edge off the morning's chill.

Two hound dogs, penned up and sitting atop an old stump, yelped and howled as I pulled into the front yard. Their breath hung in the air like puffs of smoke. My car came to a stop beside a rusty pickup truck, and before me two ancient, white house trailers sat side by side, joined in the middle by a covered walkway. A sturdy ramp brought me up along the side of the trailers to a fence which encircled the back porch.

Looking westward from the porch, my eyes skimmed the nearby rolling hills. No people, cabins, or trucks—just the darting movements of birds through the woodlands. The smell of pine trees permeated the frosty air. Turning, I rapped on the trailer's sliding glass door.

Tattered beige draperies parted to reveal an elderly woman, clad in a faded, flowered, cotton duster. Her smile, which filled the wrinkles on her cheeks, welcomed me into the home. Dry, hot forced air made me blink. Her gaunt, pencil-thin son eagerly waved to me from his double bed, crowded into one end of the living room and stacked thick with quilts and blankets. With five tiny barking dogs and the woman as escorts, I hugged the young man and settled in to talk.

This was my first visit to their home. Previously, the man and I had met for coffee at an outdoor cafe or sometimes at my office. The conversations were wide-ranging—music, politics, movies—but always included his commentary on living with AIDS. The expensive medications and their daunting side effects, the disfiguring skin lesions, the promise of alternative therapies, the pains and fevers, the loss of independence and privacy—they all weighed upon the man's mind. But despite these worries, his greatest concern was for his mother.

The man and his mother shared a closeness attributable only in part to his being an only child. Beyond that, they were bonded through an earlier life of working the carnival circuit, of lovingly caring for the man's father as he faded away, and now sharing the drama of AIDS amid the splendid, scenic, yet impoverished, isolation of the rugged southern Indiana hills.

We three talked and laughed, and the two of them finished one another's sentences and sometimes sat in serene silence, touching each other's arm or hand. They proudly showed me every item on the living room walls—old photographs, craft items, yellowing newspaper clippings, curling ribbons, a popsicle-stick crucifix, greeting cards, calendars from years gone by, and dried flowers. I was served coffee from a delicate china cup while the man grudgingly downed a can of Sustacal. His mother watched him consume every drop of the calorie-laden drink, much as I had observed my own children as they swallowed their cough syrup. "Get every drop now, we need to fatten you up," she urged him. He grinned at her, teasingly motioning as though he were going to spill the can's chalky contents on the carpet. She smiled, then stood hawklike at the head of the bed until the can was empty.

I followed the winding path to this country home several times over the next six months, and each visit saw the man becoming weaker and thinner. Infections caused him to cough violently and his stomach to toss. His sunny, optimistic personality was visible for shorter periods of time as he spent large portions of each day sleeping. Fevers caused him to awaken, his sheets soaked with sweat. Always nearby was his mother, ready to help him with a bedpan, wipe his vomit-caked lips, and hold him in her strong-yet-tiny arms.

I began to think of the two of them as the Madonna and Child. She, devoted, tender, never complaining; he, quiet, thoughtful, fragile. Sometimes I sat next to his bed while he slept and she curled up for "forty winks" in her recliner, only an arm's length away. As I kept the quiet vigil, it was impossible not to reflect on my experiences as an AIDS program director. In ten years, I had seen every imaginable family configuration and dysfunction and countless varieties of AIDS phobia and discrimination. Infected men and women told of being ordered out of family homes, disowned by the mothers who had brought them into this world. Maternal love too often gave way to stinging words, fear of contamination, concerns about what the neighbors would think, and a total severing of the beloved bonds between mother and child. Yet in this little home, the strength of maternal love was so intense, it overshadowed the monster AIDS. No obstacle was too great to tackle for this mother's son.

One night he died in his sleep. He was in his own bed, in his mother's arms, while she was whispering words of love into his fever-warmed ear. A funeral in a little country graveyard celebrated his memory, and after a time, life went on for the woman. There were dogs to tend, porches to sweep, and a new garden to plant. And despite the years that have passed since the man's illness and death, the images of that mother and son have remained sharp in my mind and heart. I think of them more often than they would ever guess. The gift of their abiding love for one another and that peaceful mental picture of mother and child has carried me through many difficult days in the trenches of this grotesque disease AIDS.

Over in That Bright Light

M. Kent Millard
Indianapolis

About fifteen years ago, my Dad was diagnosed with prostate cancer and told he didn't have very long to live. However, with good medical treatment, deep faith, the prayers of others and good diet, his life was prolonged about ten years beyond medical expectations.

Eventually, however, the cancer returned and Dad had hospice care at home and began to prepare for the ultimate healing of life, which is union with God. During the last few months of his life on earth, about a dozen or more people came to see him every day. During those visits, Dad always said something like this: "I have no complaints. Everyone dies someday since no one gets out of this world physically alive. I have been so blessed. I have a wonderful family, wonderful friends and a wonderful faith." Most people who came to see him would leave saying, "I don't know if I helped him but he sure helped me."

Eventually, we had to take Dad to the hospital because of a severe case of pneumonia. One day I was sitting beside his bed while he was sleeping. Suddenly, he woke up, sat up and looked at me and said, "I just saw my Dad."

I said, "Your Dad died thirty years ago." He said, "Really? I was just with him." "Where?" I asked. "Over in that bright light," Dad said as he motioned towards the corner of his hospital room. Then he said, "There are two of us going toward the light. Who do you think the other one might be?"

I responded, "It's probably your brother, Will." Will was also sick with prostate cancer in a hospital in Amarillo, Texas about 1,200 miles away. Dad said, "Sure, Will and I are going together, but I won't be going for two days." Then Dad laid his head back on the pillow, smiled as he gazed into the corner of the room, and seemed at peace as he looked into the light of eternity.

About two hours later, we received a telephone call telling us that his brother, Will, had just died. Two days later, just as Dad had predicted, he entered eternal life. Afterwards, we understood why he waited another two days. My oldest sister was on a trip to Ireland, and it was difficult to get the plane connections to return on short notice. However, she did arrive at Dad's bedside late one evening. I said, "Dad, Sheila's here." He hugged and kissed her, they both cried for a few minutes; and then, within fifteen minutes, he closed his eyes and entered into that eternal light. It was clear to all of us that he had waited until Sheila arrived before he took his final journey to the other side.

Later, I read that Dad had had what is called a "pre-death experience" in which he had the opportunity to get a brief glimpse of eternity before he went there. Jesus often spoke about a life beyond our sight in a spiritual realm, and I felt our family had an opportunity to experience that eternal realm personally through Dad's pre-death experience. It confirmed the truth about life and eternal life which Jesus stated in John 14:2. "In my Father's house there are many rooms. . . . I go to prepare a place for you."

Rainbow 'Round the Moon

Cherie McKay
Brownsburg

In July 1996 my husband, Bill, and I bought a hot tub. Bill's folks sold theirs to us, and it has been a blessing. With Bill's bad legs and my bad back, we decided the hot tub would make life more comfortable. It has.

Late at night as we go out and get in the hot tub, I have found a new way to be close to Jesus. I also feel near my only child, Jason, who passed away in October of 1995 of Duchenne muscular dystrophy. Each night as I settle into the hot water and start to relax, I look up and see a bright star. That star is Jesus to me, and real close by is a star not quite as bright, and that is Jason to me. Sometimes I just raise my arms up in the air and ask Jesus to come into my heart. The stars remind me of a cute story my nine-year-old nephew told. He was looking at the sky and saw a star twinkling and said to his Mom, "Look, Mom, there's Jason with a flashlight."

One night I was feeling a little blue. My husband was working in Iowa at the time, and I prayed to Jesus for comfort. I asked for a sign that Jason was okay and that Bill would be protected. I closed my eyes and prayed silently. When I opened my eyes, the moon seemed extra bright and the steam from the hot tub seemed mystical. I then saw the sign I was looking for—the steam caused a rainbow to form around the moon.

Bill and I are frequently amazed at how many nights the sky will be overcast as we settle in for our ten minutes or so for relaxing in the hot tub, and then the stars will come out just for the short period. We feel so close to heaven and have peace that our son is next to Jesus.

I find myself singing to Jesus almost every night. I might sing "You'll Never Walk Alone," which was one of Jason's favorite songs. The night before he died he told me, "Mom, I know why I'll never walk alone, because I have everyone and I have Jesus." That was comforting to me and has continued to be a source of strength at low times. Other songs I find myself singing are: "How Great Thou Art" and "Spirit Song" (refrain: "Jesus, O Jesus, come and fill your lamb. . .").

I am thankful for the hot tub and the relaxation it gives to my body. I thank God for the bright stars in the dark sky that bring me close to Jesus. Through this experience I have peace that Jason has Jesus as his savior, and I know that he is in heaven for eternity and not in pain on earth.

Song in the Night

Patricia Ashman
Muncie

I awoke very early this morning as I do so often—about 2 A.M.—and something very frightening was happening to me. My muscles had pretty well shut down, and I could not get out of bed no matter how hard I tried. This was the first time this had occurred during my seventeen year battle with Parkinson's Disease. I started to get panicky and then I heard that still, small voice and He said, "Pray!"

As I began to pray then praise God, I was overwhelmed with the joy and peace of the Lord. It was like being wrapped in a wonderful comforter. What could have been one of the worst moments in my life was turned by the grace and love of God into a very precious moment. I want to live in that joy. I can sing a song of joy in the darkest of times, and I praise God.

Can you have joy during the times of your deepest
     trouble?
Yes!!! Emphatically!!!
For joy has nothing to do with my circumstances,
But it has everything to do with who the Lord is to me.
Because He is my best friend, my Savior and my Lord,
     I can have "joy unspeakable and full of glory."
Joy . . . what a choice fruit of the Holy Spirit. . . .
It is a gift and it is mine.
It cannot be taken from me by the world.
It comes to me while walking daily with the Lord and
     experiencing His grace and mercy in my life.
It comes when I discover just how awesome my God is.
It comes when I see how much He loves me.
It is incredible to realize how much He loves me
That He would die for me.

He fills my heart with inner joy and gladness.
He fills me with joy in His precious presence.
If I lived in my circumstances, how could joy be mine?
The burden would be too oppressive.
But I choose to live in the reality of His presence and He
  removes my sackcloth and clothes me instead with joy.
And I can sing a song in the night.
I can sing a song in the seemingly impossible troubles
  of my life.
Illness threatens to overtake me and I can sing a song
  of joy, for my God is with me.
He lifts me above my troubles and carries me to the
  very throne of God.
When my body fails me,
I can still sing a song of joy, for Jesus is mine.
As I praise Him out of my joyful heart, my circum-
  stances don't matter much.
All that counts is the joy of my salvation.
All pain diminishes in the glory of His Presence.
The joy of the Lord gives me strength and I see it most
  clearly in the darkest of hours
I sing for joy.
It is a song of Joy in the night!

Unbelievers' Salvation

Linda Dunk
West Lafayette

I was nine years old when I accepted Christ in my life. Both my parents never believed in God, but a green bus went by my place and I would get on it. I discovered why I saw so much happiness on the faces of the children as the bus passed by—now I was one of the children. My mother was sick with a heart problem and my dad, a drunk. So the light within me kept me going. I married at nineteen and moved to Indiana from Canada. My marriage ended after twenty-eight years through a bitter divorce. I didn't know about unevenly yoked marriage. Yet God is good and he held my hand, faith working when circumstances showed pains of despair. God used me to minister to people. I joined Buck Creek Methodist Church in Lafayette, Indiana. It has been thirty years now since becoming an active member in church teaching Bible studies, yet my heart ached as I longed for my parents to know Christ. They wouldn't permit me to talk about my faith. How that hurt me so deep within, as that is who I am. I had asked my pastor to pray for my parents, but I felt so lonely inside as the reality of their age and health grew stronger. The realization of where their life would end up without Christ.

In January of this year my mom was put into the hospital—congestive heart failure. I called my pastor and asked her to pray. I had shared with her my parents denial of Christ.

What does it mean to be obedient to God's calling?

The phone rang and I answered it, "Linda, this is Pastor Judy, I am inspired by the Holy Spirit, and I am going to take you to Canada to see your Mom." Tears welled up in my eyes—an answer to my prayer, someone caring enough about my parents and obedient to God's calling to travel 500 miles. Yes, I was excited until we got on the road and I began to think. Oh no, I thought, my parents don't like pastors, church or even believe in God.

Through tear-stained eyes I confessed my feelings of concern to Pastor Judy. She quickly, firmly and lovingly reminded me that God was in charge.

So many feelings and actions of faith go into this story. But to make it short, Pastor Judy bathed my mother, washed her feet, held her in her arms, cradled her in God's love. She didn't quote scripture (it would have been foreign to my mother's ears), but she showed compassion as Christ would. My mother saw that in her eyes. Pastor Judy also witnessed love for my God through the Holy Spirit who resides in her.

My father and mother died within seven days of one another. What is faith? What is obedience? Faith and obedience was in the vessel of one called Judy, who listened to God's call and ministered faith and love to two lost sheep. She was not consumed by boundaries but allowed God to work through her. Words cannot convey the heartfelt love and joy of how I feel for her obedience of faith. My parents departed from this world and I know are in heaven because of an act of faith. I thank God for Pastor Judy and pray for all God's servants to obey his callings.

A Night without Stars

Harold Leininger
Brownsburg

The sanctuary of Holy Trinity Cathedral Church in Leningrad was jammed with people standing shoulder to shoulder. In recognition of Pentecost Sunday, birch trees were appropriately placed in the chancel area. Many worshipers carried birch sprigs which symbolized the coming to life of nature. In turn, the birch sprigs represented new life in the soul of the believer. The music of the choir and the chant of the priests were magnificent like an angelic chorus. Throughout the worship of four hours, I was filled with the spirit of God's interconnection of all peoples. I received the answer to the question of Jesus, "Who is my brother and my mother?" All persons, whether Soviet or American, who do what God wants them to do are my brother, my sister and my mother. In the heartland of an atheistic state, I experienced the heartbeat of God's redeeming love.

About an hour and a half into the worship service, I whispered to Andrea that my feet were killing me and I couldn't take it any longer. I maneuvered through the crowd and made my way to a side transept. Outside I sat on a ledge, took off my shoes and began to observe those who were worshiping about me, for there were many who couldn't get into the sanctuary because of the crowd. I saw a young woman who was crossing herself and saying her prayers. For some unknown reason, I interrupted her worship and asked, "Do you speak English?" She quietly acknowledged that she did. I then slipped on my shoes, took the bag I had carried to the service and pulled out an English Revised Standard version Bible and gave it to her.

Tears came to her eyes as she held the Bible close to her breast. She told me the only Bible she owned was her grandfather's which was more than 100 years old. Printed in Old Russian, the worn Bible could hardly be read. She was thrilled to have the opportunity to have the Word of God given to her. She went on to share that her parents were not believers. She and her medical-student sister, however, were believers in Jesus Christ. She made clear to me that it was difficult to be a believer in the university where one was not permitted to share religious faith. She then asked me to walk over to the cemetery adjacent to the great church, where we could speak more freely. Standing in front of the grave of the archbishop of Leningrad, she recounted her journey of faith. She was very optimistic about glasnost and the future of the Christian church in Russia.

Looking at me with eyes that touched my soul, she shared with me something I shall never forget. She said, "Not to have hope is like a night without stars."

Thank God, the nights are now filled with stars!

Unbroken Circle

Leroy Hodapp
Evansville

When I was elected to the Episcopacy in July 1976, one of the first phone calls I received was from a friend who was serving at the time as pastor of my home church in Seymour, Indiana.

He wanted to invite me to preach my first sermon as a bishop in the sanctuary where I had grown up in the Christian faith. The thought of doing so was totally unexpected, but immediately compelling.

Being a conference council director with no regular preaching schedule enabled the date to be established quickly, and I soon found myself sitting in the chancel of First United Methodist Church, Seymour, participating in worship while awaiting the moment to step into the pulpit and preach.

As one might imagine, many thoughts raced through my mind during those moments. Though I could not remember the occasion, I recalled that a little over fifty years earlier my mother and father had stood at that chancel and presented me as an infant to be baptized into the Christian faith.

And then, as a member of a sixth-grade confirmation class, I had stood at the same chancel and personally affirmed the vows taken at my baptism, and had become a member of the church of Jesus Christ. As I looked out over the congregation, I saw several others who had been a part of that same confirmation class.

Also looking at the congregation, I saw teachers, counselors, coaches and other friends who had shared many of my experiences during my high school years—meaningful experiences which had led me the year after I graduated from high school to make a decision to enter ordained ministry.

And then it suddenly occurred to me that it was in this sanctuary that the district Board of Ordained Ministry had met to grant me my Exhorter's License, which at that time was the first step into ordained ministry.

And now I sat in the chancel of this same sanctuary about to preach my first sermon as a bishop.

I became aware in these minutes, as I never had previously, that this sanctuary was a very sacred place in my life. I have preached there several times since that Sunday, and each visit confirms more deeply that recognition.

Almost everyone has such sacred places in their life and experience. They make us aware that God indeed does enter into human life, to give us meaning and purpose that only the divine presence can inspire and communicate.

Author/Title Index

A

ASHMAN, PATRICIA
 Sanctuary 76
 Song in the Night 133
ATKINSON, SUE
 What Matters 25

B

BOARDMAN, MICHAEL T.
 After Forty Years, a Prayer 27
BUNNING, JILL
 An Answer on the Sand 69
BURKHALTER, AUDREY L.
 For the Love of Mark 50
BUSS, M. DAWN
 A Miracle to Deliver 65

C

CHEN, YUNG SHENG
 The Beauty of the Scars 94

COLPITTS, NEOMA
Blessed Assurance   85
CONLY, MORRIS
Faith x 3=6   106
CORNELIUS, J.
Changing the Course of a River   102
CROSS, BARBARA K.
Sunflower Colors   80

D

DeMICHELE, LYNNE
One Kind of Genuine Miracle   33
After the Killing   67
DODGE, VICKI
"Jesus Freak"   13
From One Trapeze   90
DOUGLAS, DAVE
Candles for a Dismal Soul   46
DUNK, LINDA
Unbelievers' Salvation   134
DWIGGINS, JACK
A Tough Nut to Crack   44

E

ELKINS, SUSAN J.
The Brass Deer   8
ELLIOTT, HELEN E.
Husband, Son and Holy Light   93

F

FENSTERMACHER, ANITA OWEN
Assurance Alive!   122
FERNIHOUGH, ANNA MARIE
Leaving Is Not an Option   110

FLEENER, PATSY E.
Samaritan in a Truck   58
FOUST, DONALD E.
The Seventh Wave   22
FOUST, KATHRYNE A.
Whispering Hope   98

G

GILLEAND, JULIE
Mountain Dreams   31
GRIFFITH, MARILYN
Chewing Up Anger   28
GRING, NANCY
Mother's Hands   56

H

HAASE, PAMELA
The Bird in the Window   6
HANNA, SHIRLEY
Flowers under Snow   70
HASHBERGER, HARRY H.
All the Promises   101
HAWKS, SUE JACKSON
A Lie at the Altar   3
HENDRICKSON, JR., ROLLA B.
When It Rains, It Pours   97
HIATT, DONITA
Stubborn Streak   37
HODAPP, LEROY
Unbroken Circle   137
HOOPES, LINDA
Corn Supper   88
HOWELL, BARBARA HAYES
Praying for Parents   34

HUBBARD, AMES D.
My Angel Swims 57

J

JACKSON, JANET
Bullies 86
JARVIS, DAWN
God and Good Business 109

K

KEITH, PAMELA
Crowd of Angels 43
KOVACHEVICH, EVELYN
Night Messenger 16

L

LaMASTER, CLARENCE
Full Circle 92
LANG, BEVERLY
Coping Alone? 87
LaRUE, JEAN
Golden Circle 11
LEININGER, ANDREA
Christ as a Bag Lady 48
Bringing Church 124
LEININGER, HAROLD
Holy Hands 53
The Electric Train 83
The Last Bell 116
A Night without Stars 136
LETH, KATHRYN
Standing on the Promises 79
LIEBERT, GRACE CONRAD
Heroes, Guardians and God 52

LUNG, SR., DANNY KAY
    One True Friend   113

M

MARSHALL, JEFF
    Falling into Grace   107
MAYER, WALTER
    Lower Lights Burning   111
McGUFFOG, NEIL C.
    Summer of Separation   19
McKAY, CHERIE
    Rainbow 'Round the Moon   131
METZGER, SUZANNE
    Healing Touch   12
MILLARD, M. KENT
    Over in That Bright Light   130
MILLARD, MINNIETTA
    Stepping Out on Faith   60
    Pickup Full of Blessings   75
    A Heart for Glass   119
    A Bouquet of Trust   123

O

OLSON-BUNNELL, HEATHER
    The Kayla Connection   61

P

PHILLIPS, THERESA S.
    With Open Arms   17
PINER, AUDRA
    Following the White Fields   71
PRINCE, MICHAEL ALLEN
    Why Can't I Walk, God?   99

Q

QUALLS, MARJORIE
    Night Light   15

R

REED, JACQUIE
    Kindred Spirits   55
REIFF, PAT
    Unexpected Calls   23
RIVAS, ROBERTO SUAREZ
    I Once Was Lost   112
ROMINGER, GREG
    What Adam Really Saw   41
RUACH, SUSAN W. N.
    Every Common Bush Afire   126

S

SINGLEY, LUCILLE
    Fireflies   9
SKOC, BEL
    Two on a God Quest   63
SMITH, REBECCA
    The Right Child   20
SOMMERS, JAY
    Strong Medicine   35
SPILKER, LORETTA
    Asleep at the Wheel   5
STEPHANS, SCOTT K.
    Waiting for Hope   40

T

TEWKSBURY, MARION
    Sin of Omission   77

THOMPSON, ESTHER J.
    Wrapped in Love   118

W

WAGNER, JOE
    Amid Soldiers & Hymns   120
WALKER, DIANNE MCALPIN
    Pumpkin Pie Memories   114
WATTERS, TIMOTHY
    Miracle Girl   38
WELLS, ROBERT L.
    Heart Sparks   73
WHEELER, FRANK
    Come Home, My Son   104
WHITTAKER, LISA
    In God's Time   29
WILLIAMS, JACOB C.
    The Color of Brotherhood   82
WILLIAMS, JILL
    Hill Country Pieta   127

Y

YAKIMCHICK, DIANA
    God Chooses   10

ABOUT THE COVER

For a book whose purpose is to demonstrate how God's light has shown through the lives of Indiana United Methodists, it seemed appropriate to have the light shining through the cover in the form of colored glass. Our lives are like clay jars that have been molded by God's presence; that molding is represented with shades of glass "frits" (crushed glass) fused into human shape. Each of our "jars" is unique. In this leaded glass piece, one individual is shaped into a stance of petition before her Omnipotent Sustainer; the other is shaped into a stance of rejoicing before his Immanent Creator. Around them flows the journey of life with its brokenness, strung-out experiences, nothingness, healing and substance. Through all shines the light of God creating beauty out of all that is.

Minnietta Millard

146